JOSHUA GRAVES

THE

FEAST

Praise for *The Feast*

"In *The Feast*, Josh Graves explores the terribly important question of what it means to reconfigure Christianity as a way of life, instead of a mere system of beliefs. Along the way, we are reminded of many of the harsh, jagged edges of the story of which we are a part, which challenge our preconceived notions of what discipleship entails. But the story is not just of the cost of discipleship, but its joy too. So Josh also gives us a picture of a great feast indeed, a compelling picture of a kind of life lived in genuine liberty, and thus beauty."

—LEE CAMP, author of *Mere Discipleship*

"In my ministry on a college campus I find young Christians and old who are yearning for a spirituality that demands everything and returns joy unending. Like loaves and fishes with baskets leftover, this book will fill those who hunger after God with good things. Read, and feast on the gospel of Christ."

—CRAIG KOCHER, Associate Dean of the Chapel, Duke University

"I found *The Feast* to be biblically-grounded, culturally-accessible, and subtly offensive to the spirit of religion within me. It's because of each of these realities that this book is so engaging. Joshua Graves writes humbly, confessionally, without an heir of condescension or condemnation—inviting us to imagine with him what it looks like for things to be on earth as they are in heaven and to prayerfully contend for it to be so."

—CHRIS SEIDMAN, Farmers Branch Church, Dallas
www.thebranch.org

"At a time when it's clear that fewer in the West consider themselves to be Christians, it's critical that we think carefully about the meaning of the Jesus Story. Is it possible that what others are rejecting isn't Jesus himself—with his proclamation and embodiment of God's reign—but caricatures of that story? That's why *The Feast* is such a welcome book. Josh Graves is both a guide and a companion on this exciting journey to understand and experience afresh the meaning of Jesus' life, death, and resurrection."

—MIKE COPE, Heartbeat Ministries www.heartbeatlife.org

JOSHUA GRAVES

THE FEAST

How to Serve Jesus in a Famished World

LEAFWOOD
PUBLISHERS

Abilene, Texas

THE FEAST
How to Serve Jesus in a Famished World

Copyright 2009 by Joshua Graves

ISBN 978-0-89112-639-3
LCCN 2009029033

Printed in the United States of America

LIBRARY OF CONGRESS CATALOGING-IN-PUBLICATION DATA
Graves, Joshua, 1979-
The feast : how to serve Jesus in a famished world / By Joshua Graves.
   p. cm.
Includes bibliographical references (p.   ).
ISBN 978-0-89112-639-3
1. Spirituality. 2. Christianity and culture. 3. Christian life. I. Title.
BV4501.3.G7355 2009
248.4--dc22
                            2009029033

Cover design by Thinkpen Design, Inc.
Interior text design by Sandy Armstrong

Leafwood Publishers
1626 Campus Court
Abilene, Texas 79601
1-877-816-4455 toll free
For current information about all Leafwood titles, visit our website:
www.leafwoodpublishers.com

09 10 11 12 13 14 / 7 6 5 4 3 2 1

To Kara,
for love, loyalty, and Lucas

TABLE OF CONTENTS

PREFACE

For the last several years I've been teaching religion courses in Spirituality, New Testament, Gospel and Culture, and Christian Faith at Rochester College (Michigan) in the department of religion. I've also served as the teaching and young adult minister for a large local evangelical church. During this time, I've struggled to connect the power of the Jesus Story to people who, perhaps for the first time in American history, are learning what it might mean to *be* Christian in a post-Christian context. These students come from all segments of American Christianity: Catholic, Protestant (mainline and evangelical), and even some Anabaptists (though they might not use this word). And yet, together we've discovered that as real as the differences might be, the similarities are even greater.

As nationalism, apathy, idolatry, and indifference run rampant, I've become passionate about the project of connecting the world of Scripture with today's world. This book is written out of my struggle to live in the world of Scripture. The realms of this struggle include academia, preaching, teaching, and personal study, as well as my own journey as a person trying to figure out what it means to be a Christian, following the ancient teachings of Jesus in a modern and complex society. The Bible reminds me that the word for this is *disciple*.

I am convicted, as I listen to various thinkers (including my students), that *Christians* are in the midst of re-imagining the meaning of sacred words like *gospel, salvation, church, justice, sin, worship, grace, evangelism,* and *faith.* Christians do not play according to the rules of the world, for we are people of the Way and we take seriously the opportunity to embody the teachings of Jesus in our particular time and place. We choose the other option, the path "less chosen." The name the church has given to us for this other way is *incarnation*. We don't wage war, oppress, acquiesce, flee, or compromise—filled with God's Spirit, we are committed to enter into the world *redemptively*. One of my professors at Columbia Seminary, the legendary Hebrew Testament scholar Walter Brueggemann, once said in a class lecture, "The church always *appears* to be dying. When's the last time the church wasn't in crisis? That is the context into which we enter to do the work of God." If he's right, I hope *The Feast* will awaken heads, hands, and hearts to the imaginative vocation of being the church for the sake of our neighbors and our world.

Josh Graves
Rochester Hills, Michigan
Easter Sunday 2009

SPIRITUAL ANOREXIA

*"The myth of a return to the golden age is more pagan
than Christian. Christ did not leave his disciples with a promise
to lead them back to the Garden of Eden. He sent them to Galilee
. . . to the world of humble tasks, trials, sickness, sorrows which he
had encountered in his ministry, and to the hopes,
struggles, and expectations of common folk."*
—LUCIEN LEGRAND, *The Bible on Culture*

*"A writer, whose name I've since forgotten, once wrote that the two
great religions in America are optimism and denial."*
—KATHLEEN NORRIS, *The Cloister Walk*

The laundry list of sins I've committed—at times *in the name of
Jesus*—is long enough to cover the streets of my suburban neighborhood: pride, greed, lust, indifference, racism, laziness, elitism,
legalism, and cowardice only cover the surface. Without confession, I
would be out to sea with no lifeboat, drowning in my isolation.

G. K. Chesterton was once asked by a prominent London newspaper what was wrong with the world. He responded simply by writing
a short letter:

Dear Editor,
What's wrong with the world, you ask?
I am.
Cordially Yours,
G. K. Chesterton

Confession is the beginning of authentic discipleship.[1] Confession creates the space for God to do God's mysterious work of grace in our lives. "When we speak of our virtues we are competitors," writes Karl Barth. "When we confess our sins we become brothers."[2] In confession, God lifts the two hundred pound gorilla of guilt, freeing us to dance fluidly in God's big world. Confession allows a broken minister to stand before his church; a guilty child to stand before her father with a contrite heart. Confession also tears down the walls that divide black and white, rich and poor, Republican and Democrat, Christian and Muslim, theist and atheist. Division has become too commonplace in social, political, and religious spheres. Confession might be the remedy for which we all long.

I'm broken and live out of my shortcomings. I am the problem. I am guilty of hypocrisy, double-mindedness, and apathy. With the grace of God, I now want to be part of the solution.

—–ⁿⁿ—–

Confession means telling the truth. Humility and transparency count an awful lot in Jesus' economy. Since Jesus values truth-telling, we must tell the truth about the state of Christianity in the West. As I've pointed out in regard to my own life, the soul of American Christianity is malnourished. We are in constant need of having our imaginations raised from slumber. Feasting together on the words and stories of Scripture is the way this happens. If I'm correct that America's religious soul is starving, starvation is the symptom and not the problem. The problem is that many of us lack a diet of the Gospel in our lives. We fill our hearts and minds with the junk food of social pop-psychology and shallow entertainment. Our souls atrophy because we do not feast on the teachings of God's story. The following chapters provide a few recipes.

The atrophy of Christian spirituality is ironic, of course, because the Judeo-Christian Scriptures are packed with "feasting" language and imagery. The prophet Jeremiah declares, "When your words came,

I ate them; they were my joy and my heart's delight" (15:16). God commands Ezekiel to eat the book he's been given (Ezek 2:8ff). Jesus tells the crowd that real spiritual life is reserved for those who are willing to eat his flesh and drink his blood (Jn. 6). John the Apostle is instructed to eat the little scroll which will "turn your stomach sour but in your mouth will be sweet as honey" (Rev 10:9-10). Eugene Peterson inspired me to dig deeper into this image in *Eat This Book*:

> Christians feed on Scripture. Holy Scripture nurtures the holy community as food nurtures the human body. Christians don't simply learn or study or use Scripture; we assimilate it, take it into our lives in such a way that it gets metabolized into acts of love, cups of cold water, missions into all the world, healing and evangelism and justice in Jesus' name, hands raised in adoration of the Father, feet washed in company with the Son.[3]

Digesting the teachings of Scripture is one way Christians can actually embody the good news of God in our chaotic world. In my own consumption of the Scriptures, I often see God as priest to the outcast and prophet to the religious. As I write this I live in the inoculated suburbs of Detroit. Scripture has proven to be a powerful remedy for indifference and apathy, prompting me to go into all the world as I try to heal, evangelize, practice justice, and raise hands in adoration to God, the Father.

—∿∿—

As a collective whole the church has fallen short of this lofty vision, for more humans died violent deaths in the twentieth century, the alleged height of Christendom, than in all previous centuries combined. Genocide in Cambodia, Iraq, Bosnia, Darfur, Northern Uganda, Rwanda, Kosovo, and Srebrenica, along with the devastations of WWI, WWII, and the Holocaust, crushed the optimism that characterized the West at the onset of the twentieth century. By 1930, due to war and an unprecedented economic turmoil now known as the

Great Depression, the spirit of progress began to give way to a spirit of disillusionment.

Modern Christianity did not fare well because it failed to feast primarily on Jesus and Christian Scripture. Many of the aforementioned atrocities took place in "Christian" nations or nations closely affiliated with the Christian religion (including Nazi Germany, which at the rise and reign of Hitler's Third Reich, was overwhelmingly Lutheran).[4] Or, in the words of one poet: "After two thousand years of [Christian] mass / We've got as far as poison-gas."[5]

The following statistic reinforces my claim that American/Western Christianity is in a state of decline: according to Alister McGrath, though almost two-thirds of all Christians lived in the West in 1900, two-thirds of all Christians in the world now live *outside* the West. Hence the phrases in popular parlance regarding the seismic shift in religion as we know it—the United States is now *post*-Christian and *post*modern.

In the last fifty years, Christianity shifted to the far corners of the world: China, South America, and Africa. Scholars now note that there are more Anglicans in Africa, for instance, than in all of Great Britain.[6] The largest Christian congregation in the U.K. is Kingsway International Church, started by two African leaders, and Africa now boasts more Christians than the United States. Conservative estimates indicate that less than one half of one percent of China is Christian, though as one spiritual guide points out, "one half of one percent of *infinity* is a lot of people."

My own religious tribe, Churches of Christ from the American Restoration Movement, has been slowly declining for the last three decades.[7] This trend mirrors what's happening in most of Western Christianity, which—with the exception of two major segments of Protestant faith, Pentecostalism and Independent/Community Churches—is in a season of stagnation and severe deterioration.

Yet just as so many are losing the faith that has been a source of comfort and direction in ages past, more chaos marks the twenty-first century global landscape. The devastation of America's 9-11, the Indian Ocean tsunami, tragic earthquakes in Pakistan and Kashmir, the horror of Hurricane Katrina, and the latest surge of wars in the Middle East should cause Christians to ask two important questions: "Is God *present* and *working* in the face of such pressing evil?" and "How can Christianity be 'good news' for those who do not 'believe'?" These two questions undergird this entire book. I'm convicted that Christianity's real genius and power rests in its ability to bring healing, justice, and equality to *all* people. The real test of Christian theology is the result it brings for those who do not subscribe to the Christian faith.

—⁓—

The Feast engages the discussion of what Christianity, as a spiritual movement rather than an institutional religion, *can* sound and look like in a pluralistic society like the one emerging in the United States. Christians and spiritual seekers must continue to examine the food being consumed. That is, we need a heavy dish of self-reflection.

In an interview I conducted with well-known Christian thinker and author Brian McLaren, I asked what he meant by his conviction that Christianity was a way of life more than a set of beliefs. McLaren responded:

> I was interviewing Dr. Peter Senge, who does not portray himself as a Christian. . . . I was interviewing him by satellite. "Dr Senge, what would you like to say to to a group of Christian pastors?"
>
> *"Well, I was in a bookstore the other day and I asked the bookstore manager what the most popular books were. He said the most popular books right now were books on eastern religions. So, I want to know why that is the case in America?"*
>
> I turned the question back on him and said, "Dr. Senge, why do you think this is the case?"

"I think it's because Christianity currently presents itself as a system of beliefs and Buddhism presents itself as a way of life."

Now, that one sentence was the one sentence we'd all come to hear. It was a powerful moment. For many of us, we can't imagine Christianity as anything other than a system of beliefs. We use phrases like a "Christian worldview"—we've never questioned what we mean. And what we mean is a kind of intellectual system that has an answer to every question and a solution to every issue. Well, if you believe that is what the Christian faith is, then it shouldn't surprise you when Christians are viewed as arrogant, narrow-minded and judgmental. We've set up the whole system to give us the ability to give quick answers. But this idea of a *way of life* has to do with how we are formed as human beings and how we live our daily lives, and how we see our very being transformed and changed. That, to me, is what Dr. Senge was doing . . . he was calling us back to Jesus because that's what his followers were first called, followers of *The Way*.[8]

I share Brian's passion here. It's why I want to help you re-imagine Christianity as a way of life. It's why this book, in this order, is about: God, discipleship, justice, forgiveness, true beauty, unexpected prophets, hospitality, water, food, money, and spiritual disciplines.

———

Imagination, in its fullest sense, should enlarge, enliven, and transform—all of us. We face a crisis, in part, because Christians today have lost the ability to imagine the world any differently than it is.

When I was young, I spent hours each day in the driveway playing basketball with my twin brother. We had crazy wonderful imaginations. We imagined ourselves *already* as heroes and superstars. We saw ourselves as more than thirteen-year-olds with pimples and changing voices.

I was Larry Bird taking the fade-away game-winning jump-shot at the buzzer: "The crowd goes crazy as Josh Graves has just won the state championship for L'Anse Creuse North High School!"

My brother was the great point guard, John Stockton, who makes the game-clinching steal, the winning basket. This precise scenario actually occurred when we were in seventh grade, in a real game, and he chose to take the game-winning shot while the play was designed for me! (Jason would want you to know here that he's the one who made the shot, and now that we're grown up, his brother needs to get over it.)

When we're young, we're told to trust our imaginations. We're encouraged to explore and expand our imaginations, even if that means we end up on the moon! "The sky's the limit," they tell us. Until they introduce the all-too-real theory of gravity.

Something happens to us as we grow older. We begin to believe that we can't trust our imaginations after all. We're told that certain figures in our early childhood—Santa, our imaginary friends—aren't in fact real. We're told that responsible boys and girls don't practice their jump-shots into the wee hours of the night. Responsible boys and girls memorize algebraic equations and French predicates.

The feast of which you are about to partake dares you to see the world with fresh eyes. Just as Jesus' friends on the road to Emmaus recognized him in the "breaking of the bread" following Easter Sunday, we home come into Christ's presence when this food is broken, offered, and consumed.

Knowing that Christ is here, let's open our eyes.

Christianity in the West is malnourished—in need of a feast. I am part of the problem. You are part of the problem. We, together, are invited to a table to hear and digest the stories of our faith once again. This time, reading not to defend our previously held doctrines, but reading with humility and faith that God is doing a new thing among us. Reading to help us become part of God's movement.

When we feast upon the stories and life of Jesus, we are able to walk to a different cadence, for the childhood maxim of our mothers is correct: *we are what we eat.* When we eat and digest the words of Jesus, we will find ourselves energized to appreciate, engage, and serve God's world. Taste and see that the Lord is good, that God is moving and working in our world today!

PART ONE

RE-IMAGINING JESUS

CHAPTER ONE

Making Sense of the Mess

"The hardest place to live is right where you are."
—Rowan Williams

"Perhaps God has you right where you are because it's the only place he can make you what he wants you to be."
—Rubel Shelly

Tucked away in the deep confines of Genesis is a story about a public leader and his daughter-in-law Tamar. It's a story full of drama, one I cannot ignore if I'm serious about understanding who God is and how God works in our modern world.

This story—full of sex, deceit, power, and lies—might even embarrass a modern-day tabloid reporter. It should certainly make the uptight religious types nervous. The story is messy, confusing, and full of scandal. Jerry Springer can't touch this Torah tale.

Pause.

Take a deep breath.

Eat *this* story.

About that time, Judah separated from his brothers and hooked up with a man in Adullam named Hirah. While there, Judah met the daughter of a Canaanite named Shua. He married her, they went to bed, she became pregnant and had a son named Er. She got pregnant again and had a son named Onan. She had still another son; she named this one Shelah. They were living at Kezib when she had him.

Judah got a wife for Er, his firstborn. Her name was Tamar. But Judah's firstborn, Er, grievously offended GOD and GOD took his life. So Judah told Onan, "Go and sleep with your brother's widow; it's the duty of a brother-in-law to keep your brother's line alive." But Onan knew that the child wouldn't be his, so whenever he slept with his brother's widow he spilled his semen on the ground so he wouldn't produce a child for his brother. GOD was much offended by what he did and also took his life.

So Judah stepped in and told his daughter-in-law Tamar, "Live as a widow at home with your father until my son Shelah grows up." He was worried that Shelah would also end up dead, just like his brothers. So Tamar went to live with her father.

Time passed. Judah's wife, Shua's daughter, died. When the time of mourning was over, Judah with his friend Hirah of Adullam went to Timnah for the sheep shearing. Tamar was told, "Your father-in-law has gone to Timnah to shear his sheep." She took off her widow's clothes, put on a veil to disguise herself, and sat at the entrance to Enaim which is on the road to Timnah. She realized by now that even though Shelah was grown up, she wasn't going to be married to him.

Judah saw her and assumed she was a prostitute since she had veiled her face. He left the road and went over to her. He said, "Let me sleep with you." He had no idea that she was his daughter-in-law.

She said, "What will you pay me?"

"I'll send you," he said, "a kid goat from the flock."

She said, "Not unless you give me a pledge until you send it."

"So what would you want in the way of a pledge?"

She said, "Your personal seal-and-cord and the staff you carry."

He handed them over to her and slept with her. And she got pregnant.

She then left and went home. She removed her veil and put her widow's clothes back on.

Judah sent the kid goat by his friend from Adullam to recover the pledge from the woman. But he couldn't find her. He asked the men of that place, "Where's the prostitute that used to sit by the road here near Enaim?"

They said, "There's never been a prostitute here."

He went back to Judah and said, "I couldn't find her. The men there said there never has been a prostitute there."

Judah said, "Let her have it then. If we keep looking, everyone will be poking fun at us. I kept my part of the bargain—I sent the kid goat but you couldn't find her."

Three months or so later, Judah was told, "Your daughter-in-law has been playing the whore—and now she's a pregnant whore."

Judah yelled, "Get her out here. Burn her up!"

As they brought her out, she sent a message to her father-in-law, "I'm pregnant by the man who owns these things. Identify them, please. Who's the owner of the seal-and-cord and the staff?"

Judah saw they were his. He said, "She's in the right; I'm in the wrong— I wouldn't let her marry my son Shelah." He never slept with her again.

When her time came to give birth, it turned out that there were twins in her womb. As she was giving birth, one put his hand out; the midwife tied a red thread on his hand, saying, "This one came first." But then he pulled it back and his brother came out. She said, "Oh! A breakout!" So she named him Perez (Breakout). Then his brother came out with the red thread on his hand. They named him Zerah (Bright). (Genesis 28:1–30, The Message)

Let's get *this* story straight.

Judah arranges a marriage between Er and Tamar. Er dies because he's got moral issues. The writer of this story seems more comfortable than I am in ascribing death to God's judgment. Regardless, Er is dead, and Tamar now needs a husband, according to Jewish tradition. This is a little part of Torah known as the "levirate law" (see Deut. 25;

Ruth 3–4), which states that the next oldest surviving brother should marry the widowed sister-in-law in order to preserve the *dead* brother's lineage and to give the widow a place in the social schema. Onan becomes the lucky guy to take on his brother's wife.

Apparently he goes along with the arrangement publically. But his private acts of nonconsummation (for lack of a better word) have earned him his own noun, "Onanism." (Just thought you'd like to know that little factoid, if you didn't already.) God is not pleased and strikes him dead. Two dead brothers, a woman twice widowed, and a whole lot of confusion. Judah, the patriarch and leader, looks around and does the obvious math: Tamar is the common denominator. To protect the son he has left, Judah sends Tamar back to live with her parents, sending the message to anyone watching that this woman is dangerous. In Judah's eyes, she's a pawn and a problem more than she is a person.

The story then reads "after a long time," which in Scripture means the story is about to get really interesting. Judah goes through his own hard time when his wife dies, and he takes a buddy with him to Vegas once he's finished his mourning period. Okay, it wasn't Vegas, for those who read your Bibles carefully. It's Timnah.

Somehow Tamar finds out about her father-in-law's travel plans, and she decides that, if she is to get what she needs to survive and have any social value, she must take matters into her own hands. Tamar decides to play "the whore" (the Hebrew indicates) by wearing a veil. The veil points out that Tamar knows exactly what she's doing: she's seducing the man who's denied her respectability all this time.

Judah must not be the sharpest knife in the drawer, because he does not recognize her upon approach, which could be a testimony to how drunk he is. (As an aside, this part of the story reminds me of Jacob with Rachel: after all that hard work, how does he not know he's been given the wrong sister? How drunk are you when you are unable to distinguish between the hot sister and the one with "weak eyes"—a Semitic way of saying, "not as pretty"?) Or perhaps Judah's failure to recognize Tamar is a testament to how little he's paying attention. He's treating Tamar not as a person, but as a thing to be consumed.

Either way, the story makes things pretty clear: Tamar is approaching this encounter as a business proposition. Judah is approaching it as a "boys will be boys" experience. Both know what they want, and both get it. Because Judah cannot pay Tamar for her services rendered, he leaves his drivers' license and credit cards with her. Actually, the seal he leaves with her is his proof of identity encased in a cylinder he would have worn around his neck. Like Esau, he's willing to trade a great deal for a moment of indulgence.

Three months pass. Judah finds out Tamar is pregnant and becomes incensed, demanding her punishment for misconduct in a moment of thick irony. According to Torah, she could be hanged, burned, stoned, strangled, or beheaded. One scholar reminds us of the seriousness of the moment: "Criminals who were to be burned or strangled had to stand in dung up to their knees."[1] But Judah is specific: Tamar must be burned.

And then, Tamar sends a prophetic word back to Judah. Like Nathan's conversation with King David, Tamar exposes Judah for the Torah violator he really is and not the public do-gooder he claims to be. Judah has made a mess of his role in the story. Tamar is not afraid to bring his transgressions to the surface, despite her own obvious sins.

Only the Bible would continue with *this* sordid story. Tamar gives birth to twins, a familiar twist in the Genesis narrative—one of these twins will be in the lineage of King David, and of Jesus.

The mess becomes the place for God to do God's mysterious work. We still tend to think that God works best with perfect people, whose hair is cut just right, who know all the right language. But the Bible continually reminds us that God isn't interested so much in people who look the part. God's interest lies in people who make a mess of the part. People who, like Judah, are more interested in *appearing* virtuous than *practicing* virtue by protecting the innocent and vulnerable, granting justice to a widow who's lost two husbands, abstaining from giving in to lust and physical longing that turns a woman into "the sum of her parts," a far cry from the image of God that Genesis declares women to be. No matter how often we forget, God keeps working with lyin', cheatin', whorin' jerks.

This story says something about power. Those who have power, like Judah, usually act quite different in public than they do in private. The narrative details of this story prove the point. Judah only deals with his misuse and abuse of Tamar once he is publicly exposed. People in power so often wait for a public shaming to become truly authentic in their real messes of sexual exploitation, gender bias, injustice, abuse of power, public persona versus private reality.

Enron. 9/11. Abu-Ghraib. Mortgage crises. But big messes occur when little messes happen in the midst of our daily choices and actions. Adultery, abuse, betrayal, gossip, and hate. The big messes and little messes cannot be separated. Recognizing this entanglement gives us a place from which we can begin rebuilding our faith. God is interested in the messes we've made. God decides to enter into the mess, and makes sense of our world.

CHAPTER TWO

THEOTOKOS

"... [I]t might be true that sun rises regularly because he never gets tired of rising. His routine might be due, not to lifelessness, but to a rush of life. The thing I mean can be seen, for instance, in children, when they find some game or joke that they specially enjoy. A child kicks his legs rhythmically through excess, not absence, of life. Because children have abounding vitality, because they are in spirit fierce and free, therefore they want things repeated and unchanged. They always say, 'Do it again'; and the grow-up person does it again until he is nearly dead. For grown-up people are not strong enough to exult in monotony. It is possible that God says every morning, 'Do it again' to the sun; and every evening, 'Do it again' to the moon. It may not be automatic necessity that makes daisies alike; it may be that God makes every daisy separately, but has never got tired of making them. It may be that he has the eternal appetite of infancy, for we have sinned and grown old, and our Father is younger than we."
—G. K. CHESTERTON , *Orthodoxy*.

The four women in Matthew's genealogy: Tamar, Rahab, Ruth, and Bathsheba. They intrigue me. No offense, but if I'm writing this Gospel, I'm not going to include these women in the story. Not one of them is Jewish, and all of them are caught up in some type of sexual scandal or sexual indiscretion: as I might have mentioned above, Tamar pretends to be a prostitute in order to secure a child with her father-in-law Judah (Gen. 38). Rahab *is* a prostitute who aids Israel as they prepare for battle in Jericho (Josh. 2, 6); Ruth attempts to seduce Boaz on the threshing floor (Ruth 3); and Bathsheba's presence in the genealogy testifies to the great King David's acts of adultery and murder (2 Sam. 11). Yet God features these foreign women as intricate characters in developing the holy plot: all of them become inextricably linked to the birth of Jesus.

And the scandals continue with Jesus' parents.

Deep breath.

Eat this story.

Now the birth of Jesus Christ was as follows: when His mother Mary had been betrothed to Joseph, before they came together she was found to be with child by the Holy Spirit. And Joseph her husband, being a righteous man and not wanting to disgrace her, planned to send her away secretly.

But when he had considered this, behold, an angel of the Lord appeared to him in a dream, saying, "Joseph, son of David, do not be afraid to take Mary as your wife; for the Child who has been conceived in her is of the Holy Spirit. She will bear a Son; and you shall call His name Jesus, for He will save His people from their sins."

Now all this took place to fulfill what was spoken by the Lord through the prophet: "Behold, the virgin shall be with child and shall bear a son, and they shall call his name Immanuel," which translated means, "God with us."

And Joseph awoke from his sleep and did as the angel of the Lord commanded him, and took Mary as his wife . . . . (Matthew 1:18–24, NIV)

Consider Joseph, one of Matthew's leading men.[1] Matthew tells us Joseph was a *tsadiq* (sa-deek), one "who studies, learns, and observes Torah" diligently. This designation implies that he was passionate about several things: reciting the *Shema* daily; supporting the synagogue; observing food laws (no ham sandwiches); and celebrating religious festivals and holidays. Very few things could bring more honor to one's family than the status of being a *tsadiq*.

Understand Joseph's complex situation. He learns that his fiancé is pregnant. According to Torah, Joseph has a few options. If she was seduced, the Bible tells Joseph that she and the guilty man are to be stoned to death. Imagine that, the biblical thing to do is to kill them! If she claims to have been raped, she might be allowed to live, but the rapist is to be put to death. Either way, someone's going to die. Or if Mary pleads the fifth, there's that fun passage in Numbers 5 that offers another alternative: she can drink from the "waters of bitterness." If she's guilty, she'll suffer a gruesome miscarriage and become a social outcast; if she's innocent, hey, all's good. Or, according to Deuteronomy 22, Mary's parents might be able to produce "tokens of virginity" to clear her name.

But Mary's situation does not fit any of the previous categories: she claims that she is pregnant because God *wanted* it to be that way. So what is Joseph to do? If he stays with her, he will no longer be a *tsadiq*. This is crucial to understand. Joseph can honor God by following Torah, or he can give up the gift of dedication he has worked to offer God by having the courage to accept that God might want him to do something else.

Joseph trades his reputation for a new identity. He legally links two suspicious people to himself: a woman impregnated out of wedlock and a child born to a woman who is not married. Barbara Brown Taylor captures the scandal of this story when she writes,

> In our own age of people who raise children without benefit of marriage, the issue of legitimacy sounds a bit quaint, but the heart of the story is much bigger and more profound than that. The heart of the story is about a just man who wakes up one day to find his life wrecked: his wife pregnant, his trust

betrayed, his name ruined, his future revoked. It is about a righteous man who surveys a mess he had absolutely nothing to do with and decides to believe that God is present in it . . . He claims the scandal and gives it a name. He owns the mess—he legitimates it—and the mess becomes the place where the Messiah is born.[2]

Joseph offers protection to this fragile woman and child, but it will be God who glorifies their story. Tamar, Rahab, Ruth, and Bathsheba were all swimming in a story of sexual indiscretion at the time of God's divine favor in their lives, and Mary joins their circle of disgrace. By understanding Mary's social struggle, we understand that God is going to morph her messy reputation into a messianic vision, for to those around her, Mary is a *na'ap* (pronounced ne-ap)—an adulteress.

Mary emerges out of a large segment in Israel known as the *anawim* (on-a-wheem), which simply means "pious poor." Why did Mary, for instance, bring two birds to the temple when the Torah requires a lamb? Because she (and Joseph) were part of the working poor of Israel. Unlike the *tsadiqim*, the *anawim* are not nearly as respected in their social location. According to McKnight, the *anawim* are identified based on three characteristics: (1) they suffer because they are poor; (2) they express hope by gathering at the Temple in Jerusalem; and (3) at the Temple, they express to God their yearning for justice, the end of oppression and the coming of the Messiah.

God chooses to partner with this woman in order to bring God's son into the world. Mary might be poor and insignificant but she's not without a calling. Mary might be talked about by others around her but she's not without deep faith and right standing before God. Taylor prompts our imaginations once more:

You can decide to be a daredevil, a test pilot, a gambler. You can set your book down and listen to a strange creature's strange idea. You can decide to take part in a plan you did not choose, doing things you do not know how to do for reasons you do not entirely understand. You can take part in a thrilling and dangerous scheme with no script and no guarantees. You can agree to smuggle God into the world inside your own body.[3]

In Roman Catholicism's teaching about Mary, often misunderstood by Protestants, Mary is known as the *theotokos*. Literally *theo* means God, *tokos* means to bear or bring. Mary is revered in the Catholic tradition because she is the clearest example of what it looks like to open one's hands to God in the face of incredible odds and say yes, to bring God into the world. I can't help but think that Jesus' own energy and passion were passed down from his mother as the stories of his birth were told to him as a young boy, and as he remembered the song she sang as he fell asleep at night: *God defeats the powers and institutions which exploit and oppress, and lifts up the humble to reclaim a true identity* (Lk. 1:46-56). This song, known as the *Magnificat*, becomes the seedbed for Jesus' deep spirituality and his intense passion for the mess.[4]

Mary feasted on Torah. Jesus did the same because he saw the blending of reflection and practice in the life of his courageous mother.

It is only when the *tsadiqim* (perceived righteous ones) and *anawim* come together that God's way in our lives can be fully experienced and witnessed. If the hardest place to live is right where we are, then where we are is the place from which we must begin. In Tamar and the mother of Jesus we see particularly clear depictions of a God who is still about the redemption business, and we are invited to come clean and own up to our own mess. Just when we feel inadequate and hopeless, God has the space to do his extravagant work, and this divine act prompts us to deeper spirituality, a more committed life of following Jesus. Grace clears the landscape in order that discipleship might spring forth.

CHAPTER THREE

WRESTLING WITH THE REAL JESUS

"We Lutherans have gathered like eagles round the carcass of cheap grace, and there we have drunk of the poison which has killed the life of following Christ."
—DIETRICH BONHOEFFER

"So once in Israel love came to us incarnate, stood in the doorway between two worlds, and we were all afraid."
—ANNIE DILLARD

I have a recurring vision. It's not a wake-me-up-in-the-middle-of-the-night dream. It is a simple, very real vision. I'm standing in a crowd following an ancient rabbi. As best I can tell, he's Jesus.

The crowd is huge. Murmurs, questions, and awe fill the air. I can sense the anticipation working its way to each person present. Jesus turns to the large crowd and speaks, "I know many of you admire me, cheer for me, root for my cause. I am honored some of you believe in me and worship me. However, I do not need any more admirers, fans, worshippers, or believers. I'm going to Jerusalem to take up a cross. I need some people who are willing to follow me." The crowd gets smaller as people slink away. I also sneak away, waffling in my own doubt, fear, and apathy.

I'm learning to appreciate this about Jesus. On days when I want him to make life easy, to answer my questions, calm my fears, I'm reminded that Jesus is trying to form me into his likeness. I never expected a wrestling match with God, though that's where I find myself most days, and like training for a marathon, the process can be painful. Yet, when I reflect on my own journey, the process of becoming like Jesus has produced substantial fruit.

There are many ways to experience God's presence in our world. Corporate and personal worship can be powerful reminders that we were made for community. Scripture comes alive and changes the way we see the world, bringing us closer to the heart of God. Deep prayer takes us to strange but holy places. Enjoying the good creation gives us a sense of God's majesty and splendor. The arts also remove the scales from our eyes, allowing us to see the divine in our midst. Even silence, a tough experience for fast-paced moderns, can point us to higher things.

British mystics have a great phrase. To explain the meeting of the divine and human they often use the phrase "thin space," the unsuspecting place where God and creation come together. These thin spaces are the moments and places where heaven and earth kiss, where eternity, ever so subtly, creeps into our temporary lives.

Jesus is the ultimate thin space. He is born in a barn, and as a Jew, he is disenfranchised in his Roman-dominated world. Unlike Paul, Jesus isn't even a citizen in his own nation. He's from Nazareth, not exactly a cutting-edge city producing great thinkers. Remember the infamous line from the Gospels, "What good can come from Nazareth?" Jesus and his father are carpenters, more migrant workers than middle class. He does not appear to hold any politically elite position. He has no special education that we know of. He depends on the generosity of others during his ministry. He is voluntarily homeless. He is crucified as a criminal, a political insurgent who threatens Rome's power in the region and Judaism's tests of orthodoxy.

I often remind my students that Jesus is *not* a Christian. Churches would not hire Jesus. Moms would think twice before letting their daughters date Jesus. When one wrestles with *this* Jesus, a haunting question emerges: What does it say about the Almighty that when he enters into human history, he takes up residence in Jesus of Nazareth? What does it say about the very nature of God that he came to us in this specific way?

The incarnation, or "scandal of particularity," as some call it, says fundamentally that God can be found "outside the camp" in the margins of our world. One New Testament writer says it this way.

Eat these words.

The high priest carries the blood of animals into the Most Holy Place as a sin offering, but the bodies are burned outside the camp. And so Jesus also suffered outside the city gate to make the people holy through his own blood. Let us, then, go to him outside the camp, bearing the disgrace he bore. For here we do not have an enduring city, but we are looking for the city that is to come. (Hebrews 13:11–14, NIV)

Regarding this text, one scholar believes: "It is not that we good Christians take God outside the camp, outside the walls of the church. We go outside because God is *already* there."[1]

I confess I'm often guilty of what Dallas Willard calls "Vampire Christianity"—the evangelical Christian's tendency to "only want Jesus for his blood," ignoring the way he calls his followers to live. I am white. I am American. I am male. I am educated. I have a bit of power in my circles. I guess the only thing going for me spiritually is that I am not a New York Yankees fan. My confession of comfort cannot stop with me because I am not an island. I serve a local church. A church that is mostly white, educated, wealthy, and full of power. The temptation is to add Jesus to my comfortable life as insurance, a get-out-of-hell-free-card. Discipleship is abandoned for something less.

I'm not confessing out of guilt. I've lived that lie for far too long. I'm confessing because I don't think God is male, white, or American. I don't believe God uses power the way I often do. And I don't think it's God's intention that I want Jesus only for his blood while I ignore what got him killed in the first place.

A prime example of Vampire Christianity is found in a story from Taylor Branch's Pulitzer Prize-winning book *Parting the Waters*.[2] After a decade of failed attempts between black Baptist preachers and white Baptist preachers, Branch's characters decide to hold a meeting for reconciliation. Each side chooses one preacher to speak, to represent their particular vantage point. Vernon Johns, the main spokesperson for the black Church, reacts to a white preacher's sermon that primarily emphasizes the death of Jesus, the forgiveness of sins and promise of heaven. "The thing that disappoints me about the Southern white church is that it spends all of its time dealing with Jesus after the cross, instead of dealing with Jesus before the cross," he growls, as a number of the black preachers sink inwardly toward oblivion. Branch continues the story:

> Johns turned to the white preacher who had just sat down. "You didn't do a thing but preach about the death of Jesus," he said. "If that were the heart of Christianity, all God had to do was drop him down on Friday, and let them kill him, and then yank him up again on Easter Sunday. That's all you hear. You don't hear so much about his three years of teaching that man's religion is revealed in the love of his fellow man. He who says he loves God and hates his fellow man is a liar, and the truth is not in him. That is what offended the leaders of Jesus' own established church as well as the colonial authorities from Rome. That's why they put him up there."

Which brings us back to the vision I have of being in the crowd with Jesus.

I wrestle with whether I'm an admirer of Jesus in that dream crowd or whether I'm truly following his radical teachings. I feel like Robert Jordan, the brother of the influential writer and activist Clarence Jordan. Clarence approached his powerful brother, a lawyer in Georgia, to help provide some protection for Clarence's demonstration plot, the Koinonia Farm, which was created to be a visible sign that blacks and whites, poor and rich could live in solidarity. A radical project, especially in the early 1950s.

Clarence believed his brother might be able to provide some legal advice or protection to ensure the continuation of the vision that birthed the Koinonia Farm. Here's one recollection of the conversation. Upon being asked for assistance by Clarence, Robert responded:

> "Clarence, I can't do that. You know my political aspirations. Why, if I represented you, I might lose my job, my house, everything I've got."
>
> "We might lose everything too, Bob."
>
> "It's different for you."
>
> "Why is it different? I remember, it seems to me, that you and I joined the same church the same Sunday, as boys. I expect when we came forward the same preacher asked me about the same question he did you. He asked me, 'Do you accept Jesus as your Lord and Savior?' And I said, 'Yes.' What did you say?"
>
> "I follow Jesus, Clarence, up to a point."
>
> "Could that point by any chance be—the cross?"
>
> "That's right. I follow him to the cross, but not on the cross. I'm not getting myself crucified."
>
> "Then I don't believe you're a disciple. You're an admirer of Jesus, but not a disciple of his. I think you ought to go back to the church you belong to, and tell them you're an admirer not a disciple."
>
> "Well now, if everyone who felt like I do did that, we wouldn't have a church, would we?"
>
> "The question is," Clarence said, "*do you have a church*?"[3]

The chief antagonists in this mini-drama were not the conventional bogeymen constructed so often in contemporary religious polemics: the "liberals," "atheists," and "homosexuals." Christians were the ones who physically assaulted, shunned, and imposed economic difficulties on the Koinonia Farm. Baptist. Methodist. Presbyterian. Churches of Christ. It was the "Christians" who prevented the gospel from having its way in the Jim Crow South.

Every day I wrestle with *my* identity: am I a merely a spectator, or am I truly following? I stand somewhere between these two brothers— at times willing to lay down everything for the kingdom, at other times, doing everything in my power to preserve my comfortable life, career, and positions. I firmly believe that more than understanding Christianity as a "set of beliefs," ours is a faith that demands to be seen as a "way of life." A theological battle bubbles like witch's brew—there's a pinch of truth and a whole lot dangerous poison. If you listen carefully to the language coming out of the chaos of our post-9/11, post-Katrina world, we are immersed in a debate over the meaning of sacred words. The words that appear to be at the heart of the debate within Christian conversations are "Gospel" and "Jesus."

The battle I hear in churches and on college campuses all over the United States surrounds the word *gospel*. What does the church mean when it says, "The gospel is the hope for the world?" Do we mean what Martin Luther meant: salvation by grace through faith? Do we mean the Sinner's Prayer as a personal fire insurance policy for the afterlife? The gospel Jesus preached sounds strange to modern ears, religious persuasion notwithstanding.

Take a deep breath. Chew slowly on these words from the beginning of Mark's account of Jesus:

After John was put in prison, Jesus went into Galilee, proclaiming the good news of God. "The time has come," he said. "The kingdom of God is near. Repent and believe the good news!" (Mark 1:14–15, NIV)

A few things strike me when I listen to *this* gospel preached by Jesus. First, the gospel (which means, after all, "good news") is the in-breaking of the reign of God.[4] The gospel is the announcement and embodiment of God's kingdom coming to earth. While many think of leaving earth as the goal of life, Jews and early Christians adamantly talked and thought about heaven as the coming together of God with a renewed earth. Heaven was not a destination nor a place one escapes to. Heaven was the merger of God's realm and the realm currently inhabited by humanity. Thus Jesus was "back from the future" showing the world what that day looked like.[5]

Second, the call for repentance is more than a *judgment* made by Jesus; it is an *invitation* to a different way of living in the world, a different way of seeing the world. I wince when I hear the word repentance, for I envision a preacher in a polyester suit, red in the face, screaming and ranting against the evils of dancing, drinking, and modern film— all the while ignoring, in my estimation, the weightier matters of the law: racism, greed, and idolatry.

One story from Eugene Peterson's book, *Christ Plays in Ten Thousand Places*, embodies the negative connotation of the word *repent*. For several weeks in his childhood, Eugene had been persecuted in his hometown by the town bully for being a "Jesus-sissy." Time and time again, he resisted evil with good until he could take it no more. This young boy tired of turning the other cheek.

> That's when it happened. Something snapped within me. Totally uncalculated. Totally out of character . . . I wrestled him to the ground, sat on his chest and pinned his arms to the ground with my knees. I couldn't believe it—he was helpless under me. At my mercy. It was too good to be true. I hit him in the face with my fists. It felt good and I hit him again—blood spurted from his nose, a lovely crimson on the snow. By this time all the other children were cheering, egging me on. "Black his eyes! Bust his teeth!" A torrent of vengeful invective poured from them, although nothing compared with what I would, later in my life, read in the Psalms. I said to Garrison, "Say 'Uncle.'" He wouldn't say it. I hit him again. More blood. More cheering. Now the audience was bringing the best out of *me*. And then my Christian training

reasserted itself. I said, "Say, 'I believe in Jesus Christ as my Lord and Savior.'"

And he said it. Garrison Johns was my first Christian convert.[6]

A funny story, but sadly, too many of us may be able to identify with Garrison Johns, repenting because of a evangelizing bully sitting on our chests. Jesus invites voluntary repentance, as a new way of being human.[7] A freer, richer way. This is the good news part.

Many of the Jews in the first century were asking the same questions we are today: What does it mean to be the faithful people of God? What must we do in order for God to send his Messiah to rescue us from oppression? The answers they came up with were all over the map. The Pharisees wanted to clean things up: "Let's get rid of the homeless, the tax collectors, and the prostitutes." The Essenes insisted that some must withdraw, for all of Jerusalem was corrupt: "We should isolate ourselves from everyone else and create a pure society; a holy fortress." The Zealots said, "Get your tanks, guns, knives and planes—we're going to war. Then God will surely intervene." The Herodians, Sadducees, and Samaritans were disillusioned by the discussion and their options: "If you can't beat them, join them. We don't mind sleeping with the enemy (Rome)."[8]

Jesus judged these beliefs and practices and called all people to something more. He dared them to imagine the world differently. To see the world as the canvas on which he was displaying God's intent for the world in his very words and actions. Heaven had come from the future to the present in order to begin the renewal of creation. The gospel is the announcement and arrival of God in the world.[9]

The debate raging within the reforming center of American Christianity also relates to one's understanding of Jesus.[10] What do we in the church mean when we claim, "salvation is found in Jesus Christ"? How will we respond when someone leans over, in an intimate moment of honest inquiry, and asks, "Who is Jesus? What's he mean to you?" Will we say, "Jesus is a watered down Plato, handing out fortune cookie sound bites to help you deal with life"? "Jesus is the one who teaches us that ethics is about what happens below your waist, especially abortion and homosexuality"? "Jesus is the one who teaches that throwing money at the problem is nobler than being engaged in the problems of poverty and injustice"? "Jesus is the one who came to 'increase our territory,' to give us prosperous bank accounts"?

What we want is to say and to show in our daily lives, "Jesus is the expression of God who came to serve, not to be served. Jesus is the suffering servant, God's person, who shows humanity what it means to live according to a different spiritual cadence." It was Jesus himself, after all, who used the words of Isaiah, to describe his identity and his primary activity in the world.

Consume *these* words.

The Spirit of the Lord is on me, because he has anointed me to preach good news to the poor. He has sent me to proclaim freedom for the prisoners and recovery of sight for the blind, to release the oppressed, to proclaim the year of the Lord's favor. (Luke 4:18–19, NIV)

Thin places.
Margins.
Gospel.

The following story illustrates what it means to find God working and present *in the margins,* which, according to Jesus, is the preferred location of his ministry. In the margins, God and humanity come together in peculiar solidarity because Jesus himself is the pure embodiment of what "marginalized" looks like in the world.

Philip Yancey tells a great story that could have well appeared in Luke's Gospel. A young couple, with very expensive taste, reserved a space in the downtown Hyatt for their wedding reception. The total bill came to $13,000. Not far from the actual wedding date, the groom got the proverbial "cold feet" and backed out of the wedding and lavish party. The bride immediately went to the event manager of the hotel to recoup her losses. It was too late. She faced two choices: eat the loss with no party, or throw a party despite the awful turn of events. The would-be bride decided to do something no one could have seen coming.

Unbeknownst to the hotel workers and managers, this woman had previously lived on the streets of Boston. After living in a homeless shelter for some time, she got back on her feet, setting aside a good chunk of money for her wedding day. Instead of wallowing in pity over her break-up, she decided to use the opportunity to bring dignity to the least of these in Boston:

> And so it was that in June of 1990 the Hyatt Hotel in down-town Boston hosted a party such as it had never seen before. The hostess changed the menu to boneless chicken—'in honor of the groom,' she said—and sent invitations to rescue missions and homeless shelters. That warm summer night, people who were used to peeling half-gnawed pizza off the cardboard dined instead on chicken cordon bleu. Hyatt waiters in tuxedos served hors d'oeuvres to senior citizens propped up by crutches and aluminum walkers. Bag ladies, vagrants, and addicts took one night off from the hard life on the sidewalks outside and instead sipped champagne, ate chocolate wedding cake, and danced to big-band melodies late into the night.[11]

The real tragedy in the United States is not that rich Christians do not care about the poor—but that rich Christians don't even *know* the poor. If the poor were known, they'd be cared for.[12] The poor have everything to do with understanding the Gospel and understanding Jesus, who said he could be searched for and found among the poor. When we wrestle with this Jesus, not the Jesus of religious myth, we find ourselves willing to go to the people and places he went to. Grace rushes in and compels us to a life of engagement and risk. We slowly find ourselves beginning to appreciate the Jesus who once walked among us in skin and blood.

The white-suburban-rich Jesus does not exist. That depiction slowly fades from our imagination and the Jesus of Nazareth, who embodied redemptive love and radical inclusion, emerges in his place. Only then can Jesus begin to take hold of our hearts.[13]

Tamar paved the way for Mary. Mary paved the way for Jesus. Jesus paved the way for all interested in his version of what it means to be human. It's a call to embrace, by complete love, the messy parts of the planet both personal (addiction, divorce, and abuse) and communal (poverty, hunger, A.I.D.S, orphans, and war). It's a call to trust that God is doing something meaningful with the mess.

CHAPTER FOUR

The Greatest Risk

"A church which pitches its tents, without constantly looking for new horizons, which does not continually strike camp, is being untrue to its calling. . . . We must play down our longing for certainty, accept what is risky, live by improvisation and experiment."
—Hans Küng

"It is madness to wear ladies' straw hats and velvet hats to church; we should all be wearing crash helmets."
—Annie Dillard

Lunch is the most spiritual part of my day. How could I get more spiritual than chips, salsa, and a prophet? One day, I was having lunch with a group, listening to Jeff, who was bringing up everything from preaching to politics, immigration, and evangelism. I just wanted good Mexican food, but I learned that with Jeff you get more than you bargained for.

At one point in the conversation, Jeff asked the group: "Did you know the ten largest churches in the world are not in the West? They are in places like China, South Korea, Peru, and West Africa. In the United States we are impressed if a church can cram a thousand people into a building on a Sunday morning. Some of these churches have tens of thousands meeting several times a week in homes, under-ground and above."

Little did I know that the conversation was about to get more interesting.

After I sipped on some (okay, *a lot* of) Dr. Pepper, Jeff turned to me and said, "Imagine this scenario. A man walks into your office completely at the end of his rope. He's hit rock bottom. His annual salary, before losing his job, was two hundred and fifty thousand dollars a year. In a span of just thirty days, this man spent over one hundred thousand dollars on alcohol, gambling, and food. That's one hundred thousand dollars . . . . His wife leaves him and takes their children. He's lost his house, cars, everything. He now lives on the streets and in shelters in Philly sorting rags for twenty-five dollars a week. This guy walks into your office and tells *you* this information, asking for *your* help. How would you respond?"

I thought for a minute, cutting through all the weak answers I could offer. One person at the table chimed in, "I'd tell him to call someone who cares."

I immediately felt something inside saying, "*That's* not the best answer."

So I attempted to craft a response to my prophetic peer. "I would ask him if he wants to stop drinking." I come from a family where alcohol addiction is talked about openly. I know the first rule to addiction is that the addict has to desire change. "If he's serious about changing, then I can help him." I was quite satisfied with my answer.

The third person at the table declined to speculate. "I don't even know what I'd say. . . ." All the votes were in. I had a feeling Jeff was not impressed with his lunch company.

Jeff abruptly responded, "You are true Americans. I asked my friend from Africa, a pastor, what he would do, and he said he'd grab the man right then and there in the office and start praying that God would release his soul from the bondage and captivity that was oppressing him. I don't care if he wanted me to or not. I'm a Christian and I believe in the power and authority of Jesus. Sure there's room for psychology and practical treatment for addiction. First and foremost, Christians believe in the power of God."

He continued, much to my dismay.

"So, the next time this guy came into my office, that's what I did."

Apparently this case study was a real situation! "I grabbed him and started praying for the Holy Spirit to invade his life and create transformation, real change."

"What happened?"

"I grabbed the guy as hard as I could, hanging on to him, praying with passion and fervor."

"Then what?" I was quite the reporter.

"He ran screaming into the night," Jeff said with some amount of enthusiasm.

"Oh," was all I could muster. In that moment, I thought to myself, "Is this how Christian counselors are trained these days?"

Jeff seemed to be aware of my inner monologue: "But you see, Josh . . . it's not always about being successful. Oftentimes it's about being faithful."[1]

Over guacamole and Dr. Pepper, Jeff taught me that risk and foolishness are essential in the life of *following* Jesus. All of a sudden, I felt like one of the disciples, reclining at a table with Jesus, trying to comprehend the word of God in my midst. Grace calls us to discipleship. Discipleship requires risk.

Following Jesus isn't easy. I used to think otherwise. Religion is simple. Go to church a few times a week. Smile a lot and learn the right vocabulary: "Good to see you," or "If I was any better I'd be you." Any thinking person can jump into religious culture and learn the orthodox jargon and the right ritual activity. Youth group activities, small group devotionals, Sunday afternoon trips to the nursing home once a month, or better yet, once a quarter. *Easy.*

Being a follower of Jesus was like being an American. All I had to do was fulfill a few duties, a short list of responsibilities: pay taxes, attend a Fourth of July party, memorize and repeat the pledge, love sports (after all, sports is our *true* religion), listen to country music, partake of apple pie, wave a flag, know the presidents from 1950 on, and, of course, recall the words to the *Star Spangled Banner*.

Lists are easy.

Make a list, execute the list on a semi-regular basis, and there I am, a good ol' American patriot.

Scot McKnight calls this kind of Christianity (the kind that thinks Christianity is easy, nothing but roses and lemonade) "Trumanist" Christianity. If you've seen the film *The Truman Show*, you understand McKnight's point. He claims that he grew up a Trumanist Christian. That is, he was raised in a bubble, a protective dome that prevented outside interference:

> We were Baptists; the rest of the world, churched or unchurched, was going to hell. I hate to be so crass, but I'm telling you our (perceived) truth. And the reason we were going to heaven was because we alone believed the Bible as it was really taught. What was taught could be snagged from the notes at the bottom of our Scofield Bibles. We didn't join forces with any other churches, mostly because they were "liberal" and being "liberal," the Dante-like lower circle of the inferno was a sure ticket to hell. We alone were faithful to the Bible.[2]

While McKnight bemoans the fact that he was cut off from the rest of the Christian world, the same point could be made pertaining to the whole world. For many in American Christianity, religion has become a ghetto carved out and removed *from* the dangers and uncertainties of the world. Instead of the church serving as a place where people come in order to be sent, church became a retreat, a way of escaping engagement with sinners, tax collectors, outsiders—the people Jesus had an annoying habit of spending time with.

I did a terrible thing several years back—I ate the Gospels, cover to cover, word for word. I consumed, digested, partook—no, I devoured four Gospels. "Why would someone who'd been raised in church his entire life be so famished for the Gospels?" I hear you ask as you read this. I suppose my reasoning was that I should know why it was that I told the church one balmy Michigan Sunday, "I believe that Jesus is the Son of God and I will follow him from this point forward. I choose to be baptized."

When I started thinking about it, this commitment was a scary proposition. I'd rather be a fan of God. Jesus could be the mascot. The church could be the audience, and then I'd get my religious fix for the week. Or I could be an admirer of Jesus, reading a lot of books about him, learning more theological language to prove my spirituality. Or, better yet, I could become a believer of Jesus. I could memorize all his important words ("for God so loved the world . . .")—you know the *good stuff*. Then, *voila*, I'd have all the right answers.

But when I ate the Gospels, I realized there is cost in following Jesus. A young rich man who graduated *summa cum laude* from Vanderbilt approaches Jesus and declares his desire to join the movement. Jesus, to our surprise, tells him he's not ready. "You don't know what you're getting into. Do you really want to be a part of this movement? Sell everything you have and give the profit to the poor. Only then will you be ready and fit to be a part of my new religion."[3]

Ouch. So much for seeker sensitive.

I think this is why Jesus chose to speak in parables, his provocative, brief stories. Stories do something to us. They engage our whole being. They take us from being onlookers behind the glass window, to the middle of the action where the sun is hot, the ground is dry, and Jesus tells a tale, infuriating the crowd. Stories take us from everyday life into another world where we experience something more profound than rules or neatly spelled out principles, because the parables Jesus told don't represent a point, they are the point!

Perhaps this is why Jesus uses parables to shape the imaginations of would-be disciples. Remember the story from Luke 18? To a group of religious "know-it-alls," he said that the Kingdom is like two men going to the temple to pray: one a sinful man, one a self-righteous teacher. The sinner prayed hard, beating his chest, and the teacher looked around comfortably, reminding God of how good he was. And Luke's punch line is this: two men went to the temple that day, one a sinner and one a preacher. The sinner went home justified, the preacher just went home. *Ah, that's it, Jesus; turn it all upside down.*

Pause.

Deep breath.

Feast on this story.

[The kingdom of heaven is] also like a man going off on an extended trip. He called his servants together and delegated responsibilities. To one he gave five thousand dollars, to another two thousand, to a third one thousand, depending on their abilities. Then he left. Right off, the first servant went to work and doubled his master's investment. The second did the same. But the man with the single thousand dug a hole and carefully buried his master's money.

After a long absence, the master of those three servants came back and settled up with them. The one given five thousand dollars showed him how he had doubled his investment. His master commended him: "Good work! You did your job well. From now on be my partner." The servant with the two thousand showed how he also had doubled his master's investment. His master commended him: "Good work! You did your job well. From now on be my partner."

The servant given one thousand said, "Master, I know you have high standards and hate careless ways, that you demand the best and make no allowances for error. I was afraid I might disappoint you, so I found a good hiding place and secured your money. Here it is, safe and sound down to the last cent."

The master was furious. "That's a terrible way to live! It's criminal to live cautiously like that! If you knew I was after the best, why did you do less than the least? The least you could have done would have been to invest the sum with the bankers, where at least I would have gotten

a little interest. Take the thousand and give it to the one who risked the
most. And get rid of this 'play-it-safe' who won't go out on a limb. Throw
him out into utter darkness." (Matthew 25:14–30, The Message)

There are parts of the Bible that don't fit our nice, neat categories. At
times, and in this particular parable, Jesus doesn't seem very *Christian*.
The sugar-coated Bible collides with the full and deep story of a world
under siege and a God who goes to great lengths to engage the world.
Readers of this parable will find something remarkable if they are willing to dig deep.

Matthew leaves us compelling clues. The first is that Jesus is talking to a specific audience: his disciples. His audience is important
because he is talking with the men with whom he has spent time. With
these very men, he's laughed, cried, taught, comforted, and chastised.
To use a common expression, he's been "through the war" with these
men. And while these are men who at times prove to be clueless, at
other times, they get who he is. These are the men whom he chose to
spread the message of the kingdom. He is telling these parables not
to the crowds or the Pharisees, but the disciples. When you are with
family you can say things without sugar-coating them. When you are
with family you can tell it how it is.

The second clue related to our parable: Matthew gives us interesting material that surrounds this passage. In Matthew 21:1–23:39,
Jesus spends his time making the point that "something greater than
the temple is here." What could be greater than the temple? This is the
divinely sanctioned place. In a time of Roman dominance and Jewish
marginalization, this temple is one rare thing Israel can hold on to.
And because we know that Jesus is talking to his disciples about something broader than the focus of Judaism, we start to get a hunch that
maybe, just maybe, Jesus is giving more than a sermon on using gifts
and abilities.

In the last clue, Jesus keeps talking about "the end." Though he's
alluded to this before, in chapters 24:1–25:46, Jesus clearly shifts the

discussion by teaching about *future judgment*. It makes sense that the apostles would pay attention more if they even possessed the slightest sense that an "end" was near.

Throughout this story, the writer is setting us up for something powerful.

Perhaps this will help. People try to live out the life of faith in different ways. Consider one man in particular.

James enters the oil industry at an early age. From the time he is twenty–seven, he makes six figures. He uses this money to make more money. He invests in Toyota, the health care industry, and cell phones. Most people don't know this, but he is one of the wealthiest men in the Midwest. You'd never know it by the way he dresses, the car he drives, how he interacts with others, or the house he lives in. He looks typical. Most who know him, know that he is a faithful believer in Jesus. But more than a believer, he is a follower. Friends don't know how wealthy he is. And they certainly don't know what he does with his money. Only a few people know him as the person who has anonymously left hundreds of dollars in their mailboxes. He leaves cash with a note that says, "God is looking out for you." He's bailed out schools and colleges that were near bankruptcy. James supports several lower-income Hispanic families in the neighborhood where he still lives and gives thousands of dollars to the American Negro Scholarship Fund. And he makes people promise never to give him credit or tell others about his acts of generosity. He never gets ink in the paper or his name in the church bulletin. On the dashboard of his car is a sticker that reads the phrase from Paul, "To live is Christ, to die is gain."[4]

Matthew's parable is not about what you do with the gifts that God has given you. There are Christians who do things they are supposed to do and there are Christians who do things because of who they are. It's the what-comes-first question: who you are or what you do? It's really a matter of what you think you have been entrusted with. If you think you've been given "pretty good news" that requires niceness, kindness, attendance, and shallow religious performance, you'll miss the passion and energy of this story. But if you think you've been entrusted with something much more important, maybe, just maybe, this parable will cause you to live your life with a new perspective.

But what about the poor third servant? His story is a tough thing to deal with. Could it be that he misunderstands the master altogether? First, the master has given him something he did not deserve or earn. Second, the master trusts all the servants to do something risky with the undeserved gift.

Why is the master so hard on the man? After all, Jesus uses the phrase "outer darkness" and "weeping and gnashing of teeth." I don't think the master is upset because the servant is afraid. I think he is upset because the slave allows his fears to carry more weight than the commission of the master. Fear God or fear everything else. In this Kingdom, it doesn't pay to play it safe. Is God safe? No. But He is *good*. The greatest risk, in the economy of Christ, is to take no risk at all.

Jesus turns to his disciples and essentially says: "I am going on a long journey, I am going back to be with my Father. I am entrusting you with the Gospel message. I am calling you to corporately embody the Good News. No longer look at people as healthy and sick, but consider yourselves healers in a world dying of sin. Bring reconciliation to all of God's children regardless of color, gender, sexual orientation, and social class. Bring peace to a world that wants to bring it about on hell's terms. I am counting on you to tell others about me, but more than that, I am depending on you to be Jesus to the world. The Kingdom needs you to be living reminders of me in the world. Live for me now. Believe in me today. I give you my Spirit. I'll be with you until the end of the age. And when I come back I'll know who lives as disciples and who pretends to be one of my servants. I've entrusted you with the Gospel. I give you my story. You may do with it whatever you choose."[5]

When I shared this interpretation of the parable with one close friend, she reacted with strong emotion. According to her, the life she had planned was rooted in materialism and selfishness. The Christian life she envisioned had nothing to do with taking the gospel message anywhere. It had nothing to do with seeking reconciliation with people different from herself. It had nothing to do with living the life of a disciple, but could more accurately be described as taking the gifts God had given her and hiding them inside some kind of Christian bubble. But, she said,

> Annie Dillard has said that if one wants to journey with Jesus you might want to wear a helmet. And, that's what I think this parable about the talents is saying about life with Jesus. Wear a helmet! Because the kinds of people who really follow Jesus are people who are willing to be martyrs. They are willing to put their professional life in the hands of Jesus, whatever that means. They are not scared to talk to homeless people or criminals . . . or rich and important people in the name of Jesus Christ. They are not content with defining their Christianity by church attendance on Sunday morning. They are people who radically risk their God-given talents—whatever that means to us today—following Jesus wherever he leads.[6]

As we consider Matthew's parable, let's accept the challenge to be brave with Jesus' story.

CHAPTER FIVE

CAN I GET A WITNESS?

"Christians go to church to make their last stand against God."
—KARL BARTH

"A religion that cares about the souls of men but not men's bodies
might be a religion, but it is not the Christian religion."
—MARTIN LUTHER KING, JR.

Several years ago, Jeremiah Cummings, former well-known singer from the entertainment group *Harold Melvin and the Blue Notes*, came to Pontiac, Michigan—a ten-minute drive from my college campus. Cummings, formerly known as Jeremiah Fard Muhammad, left his position as a top leader under Louis Farrakhan in the Nation of Islam (the African-American wing of Islam which began in Detroit) upon converting to Christianity.[1] Cummings had come to debate two Muslim ministers, over a two-day period, concerning the reliability of Scripture versus the truthfulness of the Qu'ran. I went to hear Cummings the first night.

I was the only white person in the house.

Even so, I was treated with respect and dignity by the Christians hosting this event. The second night, a close college friend went along with me to hear another debate session, this time between Muslim ministers and Christian pastors. It was quite a scene.

There were only two white guys in the standing-room only auditorium—yours truly and Mark Johnson (who was probably wondering exactly what I'd talked him into). For the most part, the dialog was amicable. Many fine philosophical and theological points were highlighted and debated. What I remember from this night, however, had little to do with the former and everything to do with *identity*.

The end of the session was near. A middle-aged black man sat directly behind me. He stood up in front of the all-black gathering, mixed with Christians and Muslims, and pointed his long finger in my face saying, "You mean to tell me . . . you Christians . . . that you don't see who *this man is*?" My heart began racing. He was staring down at me. "This man is the *devil*. The *white man* is the devil." I'm quite sure my face was red as I slumped deeper and deeper into the old wooden pew that, thirty seconds previously, was a fine piece of furniture. Now, it was the most uncomfortable chair in the history of my small world.

The crowd grew silent. The room, all of a sudden, felt empty.

Just when I thought my heart was going to burst, an older black woman put her arms around me and said with great passion, "*Excuse me, sir. This man* [referring to me] is *my* brother in Christ. I have more in common with this man because we were baptized into the same Lord Jesus."

For one of the few times in my young life, I felt in that moment as if I belonged to something spiritual, something *otherworldly*. Never had I been so convinced of the truth and power of the story of Jesus for a modern and complicated society like ours in these United States. Never had the words "my" and "brother" sounded so good.

My passion to study the life of Malcolm X, and therefore the Nation of Islam, had landed me in the previous situation to begin with. *The Autobiography of Malcolm X* is one of the great works in modern American literature. As a relatively intellectually aimless high school student, I was transfixed by the story of Malcolm X. His religious, spiritual, social, and political journey drew me in, causing me to reflect upon my own identity as a boy just beginning the process of becoming a man. True to Malcolm's often abrasive personality ("We didn't land on Plymouth Rock, Plymouth Rock landed on *us*."), this landmark book chronicles American politics, racism, drugs, incarceration, and family tragedy. It also brings attention to the paradoxical state of American Christianity, the fact that this religion built upon the premise of inclusion and reconciliation propagated, hate, division, and oppression.

Malcolm pulls no punches in his description of the hypocrisy of Christianity as the majority religion and its place in American society. He describes a scene from his Nebraska childhood in which a group of Ku Klux Klansmen rode to his home. Displaying their weapons, the men demanded that Malcolm's father come out. Because Malcolm's father was away on church business, his mother, Mrs. Little, came to the door, allowing the Klansmen to see her pregnant condition. The men threatened her and Mr. Little and said that they'd better get out of town because the good Christian white people were not going to stand for his father's spreading trouble among the good Negroes. Malcolm relayed his mother's vivid recollection of that night: "Still shouting threats, the Klansmen finally spurred their horses and galloped around the house, shattering every window pane with their gun butts. Then they rode off into the night, their torches flaring, as suddenly as they had come."[2]

The cold and harsh world experienced by young Malcolm is a world not unlike the world we encounter when we read from the Hebrew prophet, Jeremiah. God instructs Jeremiah to conduct a field experiment. He commands Jeremiah to go to the temple on Sabbath with a very specific message for the "people of God." He even writes Jeremiah's speech for him.

Eat *these* words.

"Clean up your act, the way you live, the things you do, so I can make my home with you in this place. Don't for a minute believe the lies being spoken here. "This is GOD's Temple, GOD's Temple, GOD's Temple!"

Total nonsense! Only if you clean up your act (the way you live, the things you do), only if you do a total spring cleaning on the way you live and treat your neighbors, only if you quit exploiting the street people and orphans and widows, no longer taking advantage of innocent people on this very site and no longer destroying your souls by using this Temple as a front for other gods, only then will I move into your neighborhood. Only then will this country I gave your ancestors be my permanent home, my Temple. (Jeremiah 7:1–7, The Message)

I sense a great distance between this passage in Scripture and the world I live in. Today, the term "prophet" is tossed around recklessly to the point where I need to go back and remind myself of Scripture's witness. Television and Mass Media Christianity present a perverted understanding of the word. Though prophets in Scripture do forecast the future, address social justice, and announce judgment, none of these is the prophet's primary function. The primary function of God's human agent is to speak the word of God (be it prophetic or priestly) to the people of God. "The prophet," one scholar reminds me, "shouts from the housetops what others will only whisper in their closets."[3]

I also sense the gulf when I consider the difference between Israel (Judah) and the United States. Many Christians have the false notion that, in its prime, Israel was a superpower, that the nations surrounding Israel lived in envy, just as third world countries might envy a more developed nation. But Israel was never a superpower. Even in the golden years of David and Solomon, Israel was a meager country when compared to the surrounding foreign nations. In fact, Christians today are quick to forget that Yahweh chooses Israel precisely because they have no power, numbers, or wealth. Israel is solely the work of God.[4]

In contrast, Christians in the United States today live in a country of enormous influence. The United States exerted more power and influence in the twentieth century than any other nation-state. When followers of Jesus read the prophets we need to remember that *this nation is not Israel.* The United States, according to the witness of Scripture, is more like Assyria, Babylon, or Rome, jockeying for position on the world stage, controlling nations for her own interest. These are the things, after all, that nations do. This should not come as a surprise. Empires operate according to their best interest.

My love for America is complex. America is one of the greatest experiments in the history of the world. Yet, the success of America is partly the result of the genocide of Native Americans and African slaves. These are the things that nations do.

If the church enters into Jeremiah's world—to experience the crowd, the smells, the anticipation, angst, and fear—the church will be nourished in new ways. It is not enough for the church to read the Bible as a dictionary or history book. We must allow it to create a world. A world that will set the agenda for our lives. A world that will tell us what to think, feel, and believe. A world that will invite the church to experience God, and in doing so, be changed.

Across the gulf that divides us from ancient life, back in Judah the external structures are falling. The Northern Kingdom is defeated. All evidence suggests the fate of Judah, its southern counterpart, will follow in the footsteps of her sister, Israel. They are no longer in the glory days of previous kings David and Solomon, nor are these times of revival as witnessed in the reign of King Josiah. Military threat from Babylon is coming. Death and dislocation are real and close. If one can imagine how the Iraqi citizens might have felt that long night in March a few years ago when the mighty superpower from the West invaded their small nation, one might have a glimpse of how Judah is feeling at the turn of the seventh century. Chaos, uncertainty, and instability.

These days are dark.

According to Jeremiah, the religious respond with self-righteous indignation. "But we are the people of God. This shouldn't happen to us. Yahweh is on our side. He's our God. He favors us. We're his favorites, right?"

If one listens carefully, one can hear the indictment placed before Israel by her God. *You are not living like the people of God. Oh, you think you are. You think that by knowing the right jargon and coming to the right building you are winning God's favor. But you're not. You're only fooling yourselves. You discriminate against anyone who doesn't have the same skin color as you. You ignore someone who has an inferior education. You won't associate with someone if they're not in your economic bracket. What about the widow and the orphan? Has not Yahweh cared for you in such a way that you would want to speak on their behalf.* Jeremiah does not bring an encouraging word to these people. He mocks them. *"'This is GOD's Temple, GOD's Temple, GOD's Temple!' Total nonsense!"*

America and Israel are two totally different places, but our American privilege has not saved us from committing the same sins of arrogance, selfishness, and infidelity.

———

Malcolm Little recalls from his youth not only blatant spoken racism but physical violence and oppression imposed on his father, a Baptist minister, and the rest of his family. Malcolm's father, Earl Little, was murdered by a group representing the Black Legion, a Michigan version of the Ku Klux Klan.

Malcolm had recently returned home with three of his siblings when he noticed that his mother and father were engaging in a heated conversation. Evidently, there had been quite a bit of tension because of threats posed by the Black Legion. Mr. Little became angry, and he walked out the door to calm his nerves. In that moment, Malcolm's mother had a vision of the danger that awaited her husband. "My father was well up the road when my mother ran screaming out onto the porch. 'Early! Early!' She screamed his name. She clutched up her apron in one hand and ran down across the yard into the road. My father turned around. He saw her. For some reason, considering how angry he had been when he left, he waved at her. But he kept going."

Malcolm's dad did not return. Malcolm recalls his mother acting nervous, clutching the children at bed time.

> I remember waking up to the sound of my mother's scream-
> ing again. When I scrambled out, I saw the police in the living
> room; they were trying to calm her down. She had snatched
> on her clothes to go with them. And all of us children who
> were staring knew without anyone having to say it that some-
> thing terrible had happened to our father.
>
> My mother was taken by the police to the hospital, and
> to a room where a sheet was over my father in a bed, and she
> wouldn't look, she was afraid to look. Probably it was wise that
> she didn't. My father's skull, on one side, was crushed in, I was
> told later. Negroes in Lansing have always whispered that he
> was attacked and then laid across some tracks for a streetcar
> to run over him. His body was cut almost in half.

The children awoke the next morning to learn what had taken place in Christian America: a group of religious men had taken the life of a black preacher in the name of God.

> It was morning when we children at home got the word that
> he was dead. I was six. I can remember a vague commotion,
> the house filled up with people crying, saying bitterly that the
> white Black Legion had finally gotten him. My mother was
> hysterical. In the bedroom, women were holding smelling
> salts under her nose . . . ."[5]

When the insurance company refused to pay the family the money they rightfully deserved, the family could no longer function. The state moved in, disbanded the Little family, pushing Malcolm's mother to a nervous breakdown. Eventually, Mrs. Little "went crazy" and spent the majority of her adult life in a psychiatric home outside of Lansing. Malcolm would never recover from such brutality.[6]

After several emotional breakdowns, Mrs. Little hit rock bottom. When she sent to live in a state-run mental institution, the children were split up, each sent to various foster homes to live with white families. "A white man in charge of a black man's children!" Malcolm writes, "Nothing but legal, modern slavery—however kindly intentioned."[7]

In the twentieth century, segments of the Christian faith got their story wrong. Portions of the Church turned a Christian family into a disenfranchised group. In the name of Jesus, many in the West acted on behalf of the powers of darkness.

Essentially, Christians living out this broken story were guilty of many of the charges listed in Jeremiah 7, especially the Christians who did nothing to disarm this perverted gospel. Of all the travesties of racism, perhaps the greatest is furthering the idea that some people are somehow less than fully human. Malcolm titles chapter two of his life story "Mascot"—for this was the best any "nigger" could hope for in this particular social world.[8] Imagine how Jesus, a minority in the Roman Empire, might have been treated had he lived as a minority in the United States.

These events as well as many other run-ins with counterfeit Christianity forever shaped the man who would become an important leader in the American Civil Rights Movement. Remember the charges found in Jeremiah 7? Hear how eerily they resonate with the biography of Malcolm X. Standing in the courtroom of God, the church could be charged with the same charges listed in Jeremiah's account. Charges of ungodly action involving theft, murder, and false testimony. Charges of ungodly attitude against the alien, widow, and orphan.

—∿—

Israel may seem like ancient history. Malcolm X and the Civil Rights struggle might seem like a fading shadow of our embarrassing past. But Jeremiah the Prophet, Jeremiah Cummings, and Malcolm X have all pushed me to examine, live, and explore the teachings of Jesus, the prophet, who dares to bring honest questions to our hearts and minds. Where is God calling us to act and serve today? What will our legacy be? Will we and our children remember expensive vacations or time spent at the local homeless shelter feeding the poor?

Digesting the prophetic literature of Jeremiah is one way Christians can understand the challenging nature of the ministry of Jesus. In my consumption of the Gospels, Jesus is *priest* to the outcast and *prophet* to the religious. Jesus mediates the justice of God to those broken by communal and individual sin (sinners, tax collectors, the unclean), but he challenges the religious for the ways in which they are trying to live out their convictions.

As one currently living in the inoculated suburbs of a large urban center, I have found the Gospels to be a powerful remedy for indifference and apathy. The Gospels refuse to let pat answers and impersonal programs stand as the solution to economic and racial division. The Gospels make a radical demand on my life to follow the rabbi wherever he might lead and with whomever he might invite to travel along the path.

The top question of the day for American churches is not whether we are *right, rational, or biblically accurate,* whether we have a progressive worship service on Sunday or whether we are on the cutting edge in our particular tribe. The top question for the Church is, "Do we understand who God is and the way *he* understands worship?" More than the songs we sing, our very lives are worship. The Living God is calling the Church to be a prophetic people, prophetic in the way Jesus taught and lived while he was among us, revealing the Kingdom of God.

I wonder what Malcolm Little would have done for Christianity in the United States had he been exposed to a different version of the Jesus Story. When Malcolm was a young teen, he told his history teacher, Mr. Ostrowski, "I've been thinking that I want to be a lawyer." His teacher's response would forever haunt Malcolm: "One of life's first needs is for you to be realistic," his teacher told him. "Don't misunderstand me, now. We all here like you, you know that. But you've got to be realistic about being a nigger. A lawyer—that's no realistic goal for a nigger. You need to think about something you *can* be. You're good with your hands—making things. Everybody admires your carpentry shop work. Why don't you plan on carpentry? People like you as a person—you'd get all kinds of work."[9]

Some people believe, I think, that the Jesus Way is outdated, irrelevant, shallow, and out of touch with the complexities of today's world. But if believers had embraced the real Jesus, and not a poor artificial substitute, they might have countered such cruelty, and perhaps Malcolm would have set the world ablaze with the language of forgiveness, healing, and inclusion. Perhaps there are others like Malcolm X around us all the time.

I have good news. If you are feeling overwhelmed and defeated, hold on. We are not powerless in the face of personal or institutional injustice. God unmasks, names, exposes, resists, and defeats such blatant disregard for the sanctity of human life. The only way we can more fully embody the Jesus Way is to dive into the deep waters of forgiveness and reconciliation.

CHAPTER SIX

No Future without Forgiveness

*"Grace is like the secret of a lover we've not yet met,
the echo of a time we've not yet experienced,
news from a country we've not yet been to."*
—C. S. Lewis

*"Waiting for someone to repent before we forgive is to surrender
our future to the person who wronged us."*
—Lewis Smedes

On a shelf in my office is a tiny cardboard box given to me by a friend. In fact, when this friend gave me the box, I laughed saying, "Thanks for the . . . box!" But when I opened it, I was taken aback by the contents of the box. My friend had written down the names of people who'd influenced my life in some significant way: J. T. Luginksi, Bob Johnston, Angie Peterson, Mike Robinson, Kara Mead, Jason Graves, and John Pleasant. These were the people, my friend reminded me, whom God placed in my life to remind me of his consistent presence.

One slip of paper inside the box reads, "Benny Theriot." He stands six feet six and is built like a tank. Growing up in one of the toughest neighborhoods of Detroit, Benny developed an edge and hardened look, though ironically he carries himself with a calming and reassuring demeanor.

Benny and I played college basketball together. About two-thirds into our senior season together, we went to Ohio to play a college in the southern part of the state. We played the game, squeaking out a much-needed victory. Afterwards, a well-known televangelist, who is on cable every night all around the world, came into our locker room at the request of our coach. I remembered seeing this man on television and couldn't believe he was now standing in our small, dingy locker room. I was curious to hear what the self-proclaimed prophet would say. Not as curious to know about his make-up job, but, nonetheless, I was still interested.

The super-pastor began to tell us about the healing power of Jesus. And to prove his point, he brought a man he told us had been blind, lame, and mute at one point during his life. He then proceeded to tell us of the way in which the man was healed and how he'd come to work with their church. Benny's reaction was the more interesting aspect of this experience. Knowing that Benny was from inner city Detroit, I was certain that he was familiar with the miraculous claims of many pastors. After all, many of the largest Pentecostal/charismatic churches in the United States are found in urban settings like Detroit.

Initially, Benny was interested in the evangelist's presentation. But he grew skeptical as the tale increased with several turns of insurmountable odds being overcome. Before the super-pastor ended, Benny retreated to his locker with a look of disgust and began to untie his shoes. I made a mental note to talk to Benny on our ride back to Michigan that evening. When we got on the bus, I sat near Benny at the front, as was our custom. We each got our own seat because I had seniority and Benny . . . well . . . he was Benny. I didn't waste any time.

"Benny, why did you disregard what the pastor said?"

"What do you mean?"

"You know what I mean. I watched you listening to the pastor's story. Why did you walk away?"

"I don't know, I guess I just didn't feel like listening." Knowing Benny, I refused to accept his answer. He was perceptive and intentional; he usually had a reason for his actions.

"Benny, shoot straight with me. Why did he turn you off?"

"You want to know the truth, Josh?"

"Yes."

"Well, to be honest, I don't understand guys like him. First, I didn't feel like he gave God the credit for the miracles, and second, well. . . . " Benny paused. "When my grandma got cancer last summer, I prayed every day that God would heal her. I prayed for him to take it away. I even prayed that I could switch places with her. And you know what? She never got better. In fact, she got worse. And she died."

There was a long moment of complete silence.

"Now if that guy can heal like that, why doesn't he come to Detroit where we have thousands of dying people? Why doesn't God make more men like him?"

This was one of those moments where I knew I would add nothing by opening my mouth. I said nothing.

Benny and I continued to grow closer as friends that senior year. Through his eyes, I realized that material things are just that: expendable and short lived. In Benny, I caught a glimpse of someone who cared deeply about people. While playing basketball and going to school full-time, Benny also raised his younger sister. More than anything, Benny taught me that God is best understood in people who look at him through a different set of experiences and cultures. God is the God of the middle class, but God is also the God of those society sets above and below me in the social stratification of things. Just like the Psalms taught me, from an early age, that God is the God of all life.

Perhaps Benny's legacy to me can be explained in two succinct statements. First, he taught me that God speaks to us through *unassuming people*. And second, God changes us in *unexpected experiences*.

On days when I have forgotten the power of the gospel, I look in my box and remember men and women like Benny who shape the way I experience God. Characters in my life become characters in Scripture. Characters in Scripture become characters in my life. The more one lives in the stories of God, the more confused the two become.

Next to the box in my office is a Bible. I have been thinking an awful lot about this Bible lately. I grew up with so many false assumptions about what the Bible was, assumptions that prevented me from feeling its power and pull on my own experience as a human. While my parents introduced me to Jesus, I had no idea what to do with the Bible. That was perhaps due to my own ignorance as much as anything else.

Over the last several years, I have rediscovered this holy book. Or I should say, the Bible is rediscovering *me*. The chief lesson I'm learning is that the Bible is the real world. If I permit, the Bible sets the agenda for my life, for I do not pretend to master this holy text. I am slowly learning to allow Scripture to master me as I consume its words, stories, and insights. On days when I hunger for God's unrelenting love, I know where I can go to find witnesses of that love. I open up my Bible, like I open up my box of witnesses.

I open up my Bible to John's version of the Jesus Story.

Tension between the Pharisees and Jesus is intense. The Pharisees are watching the number of baptisms performed by John the Baptist and Jesus. Not interested in having a holy competition, Jesus leaves the Judean countryside and returns to his home of Galilee. In order to get there, Jesus must go through Samaria. While traveling, Jesus stops at a well to refresh his body from a long day's journey.

Eat this story.

A woman, a Samaritan, came to draw water. Jesus said, "Would you give me a drink of water?" (His disciples had gone to the village to buy food for lunch.)

The Samaritan woman, taken aback, asked, "How come you, a Jew, are asking me, a Samaritan woman, for a drink?" (Jews in those days wouldn't be caught dead talking to Samaritans.)

Jesus answered, "If you knew the generosity of God and who I am, you would be asking me for a drink, and I would give you fresh, living water."

The woman said, "Sir, you don't even have a bucket to draw with, and this well is deep. So how are you going to get this 'living water'? Are you a better man than our ancestor Jacob, who dug this well and drank from it, he and his sons and livestock, and passed it down to us?"

Jesus said, "Everyone who drinks this water will get thirsty again and again. Anyone who drinks the water I give will never thirst—not ever. The water I give will be an artesian spring within, gushing fountains of endless life."

The woman said, "Sir, give me this water so I won't ever get thirsty, won't ever have to come back to this well again!"

He said, "Go call your husband and then come back."

"I have no husband," she said.

"That's nicely put: 'I have no husband.' You've had five husbands, and the man you're living with now isn't even your husband. You spoke the truth there, sure enough."

"Oh, so you're a prophet! Well, tell me this: Our ancestors worshiped God at this mountain, but you Jews insist that Jerusalem is the only place for worship, right?"

"Believe me, woman, the time is coming when you Samaritans will worship the Father neither here at this mountain nor there in Jerusalem. You worship guessing in the dark; we Jews worship in the clear light of day. God's way of salvation is made available through the Jews. But the time is coming—it has, in fact, come—when what you're called will not matter and where you go to worship will not matter.

"It's who you are and the way you live that count before God. Your worship must engage your spirit in the pursuit of truth. That's the kind

*of people the Father is out looking for: those who are simply and hon-
estly themselves before him in their worship. God is sheer being itself—
Spirit. Those who worship him must do it out of their very being, their
spirits, their true selves, in adoration."*

*The woman said, "I don't know about that. I do know that the
Messiah is coming. When he arrives, we'll get the whole story."*

*"I am he," said Jesus. "You don't have to wait any longer or look any
further."* (John 4: 7–26, The Message)

The disciples couldn't make sense of Jesus' actions. Why does he
associate with such a woman? The woman, however, fully understands
what is happening. She leaves in such a hurry that she leaves her jar
behind. She returns to the village (where I'm quite sure her reputation
was less than stellar) to bear witness to the man at the well who knew
her inside and out. A man who just might be the Messiah. Jesus liber-
ates her from her sin, darkness, past, and reputation. In this one story,
Jesus deconstructs the barriers of race, gender, politics, religion, and
geography—challenging me to consider the same barriers I run into in
urban and suburban America.

This seeker-turned-evangelist, the woman at the well, is intentionally placed in this moment of John's Gospel narrative. The contrast is
strong. Don't miss what's happening, for in chapter John presents:

A man

A man *with a name*, Nicodemus

A man with a name *who happens to be Jewish*

A man with a name who happens to be Jewish *and a Pharisee*

A man with a name who happens to be a Jewish Pharisee:

   respected, with authority, and educated

A man who comes by night

Asking deep theological questions

Leaving more confused than when he came.

And in chapter four, John presents:

A *woman*

A woman *with no name*

A woman with no name *who's considered an ethnic half-breed*

A woman who is a religious heretic

A Samaritan with no education

And *Jesus comes to her* by daylight

Jesus asks her questions

She leaves the conversation as the first evangelist in the entire story.

It seems this woman found, not what she'd been searching for that particular day (water and anonymity), but rather what she'd been searching for her entire life. *Unassuming people and unexpected experiences.* This is where God shows up.

Jesus teaches the disciples a scandalous lesson about grace here. This story reminds me that people are more important than principles. This is, after all, what Jesus meant when he taught that the *entirety* of Torah hangs upon "loving God and loving neighbor."

Evil and sin are not "out there" residing in "those folks." Rather, evil and sin run right through the middle of *me*. The "us" and "them" *demonization* that characterizes so much of our political, social, and religious life (tribalism) is a smoke-screen created to divert our attention from the real matter at hand: the man or woman staring back in the mirror. Until we see ourselves as participating members of dysfunction, sin, and injustice, we cannot move through the redemptive process of healing and change. Gandhi's words ring true: *we must become the change we desire to see in the world.*

Bishop Desmond Tutu provides a concrete and contemporary way to engage the subject of sin in healthy and life-affirming ways.[1] Bishop Tutu is most known for his appointment to the Truth and Reconciliation Commission, or TRC, by South African icon and leader extraordinaire, Nelson Mandela. An ordained priest, Tutu was able to accomplish in South Africa, in the immediate wake of apartheid's death and destruction, what some Christian scholars are calling the most important Christian contribution of the twentieth century.

Apartheid, simply understood as the legal separation of people based on race and skin color, flourished in South Africa for much of the twentieth century. It was a brutal system employed by a powerful white minority to control a disempowered black majority. "You know you've created God in your own image," writes Anne Lamott, "when God hates all the same people as you." Tutu's landmark recollection of the Apartheid Era in South Africa, *No Future Without Forgiveness*, is loaded with stories that illustrate the injustice and sins committed by humanity against humanity. Consider the story of Zahrah Narkedien, a female survivor of apartheid's brutality and disdain for human dignity.[2]

This story haunts me.

Zahrah Narkedien is a black citizen of South Africa. She is falsely accused of involvement with a car bomb near the Durban beachfront. She is arrested and detained. Her hands are cuffed and her head is covered. She cannot see. She remains in a vehicle for three hours. Her blindfold is soaked with sweat. Narkedien is tortured and questioned. For seven days in a row she is treated as an animal. "When they hurl abuse at her," Tutu writes, "she rolls the rosary beads in her hand . . . and prays silently."

Narkedien is moved to solitary confinement. She refuses to break or give in to the violent tactics of her oppressors. She affirms her innocence and does not offer the coerced confession they seek. Realizing that Narkedien is unusually resolute, the torture intensifies, for she is now seen as a woman in a man's world, relegated to the status of animal, subhuman. Her jailers, she says, "threatened to go back to my house where my sister was staying with me and kidnap my four-year-old nephew Christopher, bring him to the thirteenth floor and drop him out of the window." And then the torturers insisted on having a woman present, because they were planning to increase their physical abuse to dangerous levels:

> All these days I was wearing the same clothing, just a dress, and
> I was also menstruating at that time. . . . And I was bleeding a

lot. They made me lie on the floor and do all kinds of physical exercises, lifting my body with my hands, what they call press-ups, then reducing the fingers until I had to pick myself up with just two fingers. By then I couldn't because my body was tired, it was sore and I had to drop it and lift it up and I was hurting my knees every time I dropped it. While I was down they would kick me and tramp on me. . . ."

Narkedien never received a fair trial, and because she would not confess to a crime she was not responsible for, she was sentenced to prison for several years.

I don't even want to describe psychologically what I had to do to survive down there. I will write it one day, but I could never tell you. But it did teach me something. . . that no human being can live alone. . . because there's nothing you can do to survive all by yourself. . . . I felt as the months went by that I was going deeper and deeper into the ground. . . . As the months of isolation went by I used to feel that God had abandoned me, the whole world had abandoned me, I was totally alone in the universe. . . .

And after her release, her experiences still refused to leave her alone:

I struggle to be normal, the more disturbed I become. I had to accept that I was damaged, part of my soul was eaten away as if by maggots, horrible as it sounds, and I will never get it back again.[3]

I read Narkedien's account over and over again, hypnotized, at first unable to believe that such evil could prevail in one of our so-called sophisticated nation-states.

From a distance, in my safe office, in my safe neighborhood, I am overwhelmed with grief for the death and decay that consumes women, men, and children like Narkedien. I'm also overwhelmed by the great irony of apartheid in South Africa, which was funded and executed by persons professing allegiance to Jesus of Nazareth—primarily, those in the Dutch Reformed Church. Equally ironic, and a source of hope, is the reality that different sects within Christianity—including the Catholic, Anglican, and Methodist communities—came along to speak truth to the violence being carried out by women and men sharing the same religious name: Christian.

The parallel to America's demons of racism and classism is stark and undeniable. The story of Malcolm X, for instance, is a strong reminder of Christian failures in the United States. During the time of slavery's presence in God's "New Israel," Americans pretended to believe that *all men were created equal with certain inalienable rights.* Today, we are still reaping the results of our own injustice. We need not look very far back in the rearview mirror to see our sins.[4]

The story of Jesus meeting the woman at the well is *our* story, *my* story. I find it amusing that many people, especially the affluent and powerful, place themselves in the "Jesus" role when reading stories like this one. We are not Jesus in every story. We are the ones to whom Jesus comes.

We need our sins named so that we can be brought to God's place of healing. In light of the U.S. infatuation with separating church and state, it's interesting that Bishop Tutu never apologized for bringing the Christian message of radical grace and reconciliation to the Truth and Reconciliation Commission's processes to attain justice. He delivered the Jesus Feast to them when they were hungry and in need.[5] In fact, he knew as a result of his own training and experience that if he was to lead the TRC, he could only do so out of the conviction that sin needed to be named and forgiven by the victims as well as the perpetrators. Tutu writes that the further removed he was from the events of apartheid and his work with the TRC, "it was a relief to discover that in fact we were all really children of Adam and Eve." He continues:

When God accosted Adam and remonstrated with him about contravening the order God had given about not eating a certain fruit, Adam had been less than forthcoming in accepting responsibility and disobedience. No, he shifted the blame to Eve, and when God turned to Eve, she too had taken a leaf from her husband's book (not the leaf with which she tried ineffectually to hide her nakedness) and tried to pass the buck. We are not told how the serpent responded to the blame pushed on it. So we should thus not have been surprised at how reluctant most people were to acknowledge their responsibility for the atrocities done under apartheid. They were just being descendants of their forebears and behaving true to form in being in the denial mode or blaming everyone and everything except themselves. Yes, it was all in our genes. "They" were to blame. There we go again, showing ourselves as true descendants of our first parents.[6]

Slavery, genocide, avarice, gender discrimination, unjust wars, exploitation, and infidelity can only be dealt with when they are brought from the darkness of secrecy into the light of transparency. This only happens by the practice of confession, the naming and forgiving of sins.

Humans all too easily become the very thing we claim to be against. Our fear and anger in reaction to the monster often acts as a catalyst in causing us to become monsters ourselves. As Bishop Peter Storey, another survivor of South African apartheid, reminds us, "One of the tragedies of life, sir, is it is possible to become like that which we hate most . . . ."[7] I'm struck by the way American preacher and novelist Frederick Beuchner articulates this same truth:

> To lick your wounds, to smack your lips over grievances long past, to roll over your tongue the prospect of bitter confrontations still to come, to savor to the last toothsome morsel both the pain you are given and the pain you are giving back—in many ways it is a feast fit for a king. The chief drawback is that what you are wolfing down is yourself. The skeleton at the feast is you.[8]

The story of the woman at the well and the work of Desmond Tutu collide with contemporary culture in unexpected ways. Regardless of one's ethnicity, socioeconomic status, or religion, we find ourselves in a world bent on competition, revenge, and the preservation of individual rights. This was true in the first-century world of Jewish rabbis and scandalous women. It is just as true now in our world of Christians versus Muslims, whites versus black, red state versus blue state, us versus them.

Jesus calls the church to be God's "future on display in the present," showing the justice of Jesus in counter-cultural ways. The global church, like all society, has no desirable future without the intentional practice of forgiveness and reconciliation. This is where the Western judicial system often falls short. While jail sentences are dispersed and large sums of monies sometimes allotted, the real issue at stake is not addressed. We treat the proverbial symptom, ignoring the disease. More important than sums of money or prison sentences is the need for reconciliation between flesh-and-blood humans whose eyes must meet despite the pain boiling inside.

We are all guilty. We are all sick. We have all broken relationship with fellow humans and with God. Our sins desperately need naming. We desperately need forgiving.

The only way this grand reconciliation-vision occurs is when individuals decide to take note of the extravagant grace that God laces into the everyday experiences of our lives. Reconciliation will only be possible if, one by one, people decide to lay down revenge and rights for relationship. Christians not only should be joining this conversation, we should be the catalysts for such dialog to occur in the first place.[9]

Unassuming people and unexpected experiences usher the cosmic reality of sin and grace into the forefront of our everyday lives. When properly understood and applied, grace is disorienting and shocking. If it isn't scandalous, it probably isn't grace. C. S. Lewis was once asked, at the onset of an inter-faith dialog in London, about what separated

Christianity from the various religions of the world. "That's easy," remarked Lewis, "grace."[10]

Easy to say. Difficult to practice.

Many believe that talk of sin and forgiveness, open truth-telling and reconciliation are passé, tools of an era long past. But sin in many ways is our last best hope, for we have no future without the awareness of sin and the power of forgiveness.

CHAPTER SEVEN

SUFFERING CAN BE BEAUTIFUL

*"My illusions of solving the problems of this country have
long ago left me. They have been replaced with the hope of a
risen savior who understands what it means to suffer in this
world. This world refuses to work on God's terms and thus will
always be filled with suffering. And because I live in this world,
I am privy to that suffering whether I am living in America or
Uganda. While I will never stop trying to eliminate the suffering
in this world, the suffering in Uganda, the suffering in losing
a younger sister to A.I.D.S, or even the suffering in my own
life, I do not believe that is all I should be doing. Solutions are
wonderful. Cures are amazing. Answers are great. But in this
broken world, I am beginning to believe we need more people
who are willing to enter into the suffering of others whether
they can help or not. I want to choose to suffer for the sake of
others. I am not always sure how to do that or what it looks like,
but most days I wake up and can't think of anything else to do.
Uganda has problems, I pray that God will solve them, but until
He does I will also pray for the strength to suffer."*
—ADAM LANGFORD, missionary in Uganda,
written weeks before he died in an auto accident

Greg is a brilliant man. In graduate school he studied under Luke
Timothy Johnson, one of the leading theologians and New
Testament scholars in the world, at Emory University in Atlanta. Greg

is unassuming and reserved, and he is a true man of God, with a rare presence and sensibility.[1]

Sally is an energetic, passionate, and dedicated mother. Her smile and sense of humor are contagious. My wife describes Sally as "joyful, sweet, and welcoming—the kind of person you love to be around." Upon first meeting her, you'd never know Sally survived a dangerous childhood in Laos.

Greg grew up in a Christian home with godly parents and siblings. He claims to have grown up in a protective bubble because he's never understood the concept *dysfunctional family*. He assumed everyone's experience was his experience. Though a stellar basketball player, he avoided the high school party scene by spending time with his two best friends, eating pizza, watching movies, and playing games on Friday nights while classmates were up to other things.

From an early age, Greg decided he wanted to enter Christian ministry; he never wavered from this commitment. He attended a Christian liberal arts college in Arkansas where he studied Greek and Hebrew. He then attended seminary in Memphis, which propelled him to earn a Ph.D. in New Testament. From there, Greg moved to a different liberal arts college to teach religion and culture.

"I lived a focused, simple, and sheltered life," he said. "And I didn't understand any other kind. Because of that, I began at times to wonder what other lives were like. I began to fantasize about the kind of person I would like to date. When I did, I imagined someone as completely different from me as possible. I remember thinking first how much fun it would be to date someone who was from another country. But then, to make it even better, I thought it would be cool if the person didn't speak English as their native language. Finally, in my fantasy quest to find someone as completely different from me as possible, I thought it would be even better if, on top of all this, she was a communist defector."

Shortly after having this revelation, a friend introduced Greg to a fellow student named Saysavad Phengsom (Sally). After a brief time of getting to know each other—he says "courting," Sally says "stalking"— the two went to the movies to watch a new James Bond movie.

"So what brought you to America?" Greg asked Sally.

"Freedom," she replied.

Sally (much easier to pronounce than Saysavad Phengsom) was born in Laos, near Thailand and Vietnam. Coming from a family with seven children, Sally learned to work hard from an early age: her mother farmed while her father worked odd jobs for wealthy Americans. Sally's childhood could not have been more different from Greg's.

"While I was spending my formative years playing *Risk* with friends or watching movies," says Greg, "Sally would go down to the river with friends to hunt for clams, mussels, and fish to feed her family. One very hot day Sally decided to take a break and sit under a tree. Her friends went on without her as she fell asleep. She was woken up later by a hissing sound. She looked around in every direction, but saw nothing. Finally she looked up and hanging down over her head was a giant cobra with its back arched and ready to strike. She prayed that the snake wouldn't bite her or, if it did, that she would at least make it home in time to see her family before she died. Slowly she crawled out from under the tree until about ten feet away and then ran."

Communists took over Laos in the mid-1970s, putting Sally's father in the center of investigation under the watchful eye of Laos' now suspicious leadership. Her father came under the suspicion of those who resented any American influence. Sally was eight years old at this time. Fear pierced the family, according to Sally, because many of the Americans they knew were either incarcerated or ended up committing suicide. The physical threat was enough to convince Sally's father that he needed to escape to neighboring Thailand. He eventually made it there, though he was shot at in the process. Sally's mother was left to care for seven children on her own.

Life under communism wasn't easy. Soldiers watched their house, believing that her father would return. They were not allowed to have visitors and could only travel to the doctor, school, and market. A few years later, Sally's mother decided that she was also going to attempt to leave Laos. Her husband had given her strict instructions that if she were to come, she'd better bring the entire family. No one could be left behind.

After several attempts to leave, the family finally caught a break. A man they had not known before came to them with a plan for escaping to Thailand. The next day was devoted to preparation, though none of the children knew—they just spent the day cleaning and doing laundry. Later that night, their time came.

A white car came to pick them up without fanfare or warning. The driver removed his hat as the definitive gesture. Sally's mother took her children and got into the car, and they drove several hours toward the jungle. After a long walk, the scared and frantic family joined a large group of other citizens of Laos on the run. A small band of men, fully armed, led the group through the jungle. With nothing to eat, no water to drink, these survivors waited until dark to make their trek through the unknown elements of the jungle.

Fear paralyzed them. One wrong move and the Communist regime would execute all of them for attempting to flee. "At one point," Greg tells me, "Sally's two-year-old sister began to cry. One of the armed guides instructed Sally's mother to keep the child quiet. If she failed to do so, he said, 'I'll kill her.'"

Eventually the motley crew made it close to the Mekong River, on the edge of the border between Laos and Thailand. The walkers had to be extra careful as they were near unmarked minefields. Sally's mom, paralyzed to the core with fear, passed out. Others helped her and she regained consciousness. As the group came toward the bank of the river a light flashed as a symbol of rescue. A man with a boat came to them. Packed beyond belief, the boat took three times the normal time to cross the river.

Once they entered Thai soil, danger was still paramount. The family hid from Thai soldiers who could "rob, rape, kill, or send them back to Laos." Eventually, the family of eight made it to the same refugee camp where their father awaited them with much joy and relief.

The family remained in the refugee camp, a rough and violent community not all that different from a makeshift prison, for two years. People from Laos, Cambodia, China, and Thailand all inhabited this community. After two years of poverty, hunger, and danger, the entire family secured seats on a plane heading to America. When they arrived, they were met at the airport by a group of people who were chosen to sponsor their family. These sponsors were three families from a church in New Jersey.

Though this story is filled with suffering, their pain has since been transformed into peace and solidarity. Sally reminds me of a truth that holds the universe together: suffering can be redemptive. It can be beautiful. Despite our natural reflex to avoid and gloss over suffering, it can be the means by which all is made whole and right. Time and time again, humans prove that we have the ability to take on the strength of that which we overcome.

A few years ago an article was published in a popular American magazine entitled, "The Foot Is the New Hand." The article stated that Americans traditionally spent more money on manicures and hand products, but that now the industry that cares for feet is as lucrative as the industry that cares for hands. We purchase scrubs, lotions, and pedicure sets to pamper our toes and feet. Customers go into the salon just for a pedicure and are more concerned with how beautiful their feet are than their hands.

Just for the record, I tend to stay away from magazine articles pertaining to our appendages. My friend, Sara, brought this article to my attention. At the time Sara read the article, she told me, she looked down at her feet in dismay. Her feet stood no chance in the new fad. She'd just run the Detroit Marathon.

If you've never seen a real runner's feet, you've never seen how ugly feet can become. Feet pounding the pavement for twenty-six miles take a beating. At some races, there are ugly feet contests in addition to the race. These contests feature male and female winners of the ugliest feet, as well as winners in the black toenail division.

During her first marathon, Sara lost two toenails. She was a new runner and wore really bad shoes. The second time she ran a marathon, this one in Detroit, she got better shoes and didn't lose toenails. Instead they just turned black and bruised and incredibly hard.

Calluses, blisters, dirt, and grime: it's not a pretty picture.

I can relate to this description. A few years ago, I ran my first marathon. I had calluses on my feet in places I'd never paid attention to before. My heels were worn down. Blisters bulged out of the tops of my toes. My toenails still have not recovered.

Keep that picture in your mind as you consider Isaiah 52:7: *"How beautiful on the mountains are the feet of those who bring good news, who proclaim peace, who bring good tidings, who proclaim salvation, who say to Zion, 'Your God reigns!'"* (NIV).

Every person who reads this book faces battles. Not only do we not see feet as beautiful, we are tempted to think and talk as if God isn't in the *reigning* business anymore. At a church I belonged to a few years ago, we buried a nineteen-year-old artist who succumbed to a long battle with drug addiction. We had prayed for him and his family. Many of those prayers took place just hours before he overdosed. That dark Monday morning, I walked into the apartment where his body lay cold and dead. It was difficult to see God's power in that moment.

Many religious people find themselves living in broken relationships, amidst homes and lives where the forces of evil seem to be toying with them. In the midst of the confusion of human relationships, even Christian relationships, it is often difficult to see God as reigning.

In the midst of all our battles, we need to close our eyes and envision the Good News. I hold on to the belief that the battles of this world are not the final answer. I hold onto the message that "God reigns."

This passage from Isaiah emerges out of an pivotal time in Israel's history. Israel's army was fighting far away from their home turf. Israel waited expectantly for news of battle. But this was before the convenience of Anderson Cooper reporting for CNN. In ancient Israel, battles took place far away, and those at home could do nothing but wait and pray.

When an army won or lost a battle, messengers ran for days to bring news back to the people at home. This was before the days of Nike running shoes, too, and these runners probably ran with bare feet. Pounding the ground with news that would create celebration— or news that could create chaos.

Israel waited for this messenger, some in watchtowers, their stomachs nervous and their palms sweaty. Perhaps their hearts beat rapidly as they waited to learn if the messenger's news was good or bad. Their eyes scanned the figure in the distance for any sign that he bore victory or defeat in his demeanor. The messenger might use his last bit of energy to fall in front of those waiting for him, and when the outcome was favorable, he announced, "Peace."

He announced, "Good news." He announced, "Victory." He announced the words they longed to hear: "God reigns."

This salvation business was not individually focused—it was news for the whole group. And the people likely rejoiced together as they picked up this tired guy and carried him to comfort. And as they looked down at his feet, which had just traversed many miles, barefoot, over sand and rock, those feet could not have been anything but ugly.

Yet the prophet declares, "How *beautiful* upon the mountains are the feet of the messenger who announces peace, who brings good news." The good news they celebrated in Isaiah was about military victory, but for the whole of Israel's history, it was also about salvation and their relationship with God. They saw the military victory as a sign of God's love for them, of his favor in their lives, of his reign in the world. This was more than a military victory. This news solidified God's message, the one he'd been speaking for a long time.

God wanted Israel to know he loved them. In the context, leading up to chapter 52, the reader is reminded of these truths:

Even though you looked to other gods (48:5),

Even though you put your trust in idols (48:14),

Even though you rebelled from birth (48:8),
Even though I must refine you with my discipline and justice
     (48:10),
Even though you chose darkness over light (50:11),
Even though I called and you did not answer me (50:2) . . .
Despite all of this, I love you, Israel. I have not forsaken you.
Israel, I have engraved you on the palms of my hands (49:16).

Engraved on the palms of God's hands. What an image of force and intimacy! I know of one person, a former missionary doctor in Africa, who in response to this idea had names for God tattooed on the palms of his hands.

God loves Israel and wants them to experience that love as a sign of his love and mercy for the rest of the world. Israel is not an exclusive club—they are to be witnesses to those who've not seen and heard the mighty deeds of Yahweh. "Your God reigns," the messenger said. "Yahweh Malach." "God is King." The importance of this truth to the life of Israel is evidenced throughout the Psalms as we see Israel incorporating God's reign into their worship.

"Yahweh Malach" sounds like an Old Testament phrase, yet it doesn't end with the Old Testament. Mark's Gospel, especially, uses much of this same vocabulary. The New Testament Gospels as they report the life of Jesus Christ on earth go beyond the Old Testament understanding of "Yahweh Malach" and further clarify what it means when Christians declare "The Lord reigns."

Eat the words of Mark 1:14–15:

After John was put in prison, Jesus went into Galilee, proclaiming the good news of God.

"The time has come," he said. "The kingdom of God has come near. Repent and believe the good news!" (NIV)

Sound familiar? It's the *gospel*. The good news, brought not from a mere messenger, but from God himself. There were many who did not get it then, and there are many who do not get it now.

If you ask a child to draw a picture of a king, you'll probably get a fairly predictable result. Actually, you'll probably get the same result if you ask an adult to do the same thing. *King* equals *glory and power and beauty*. Jesus came into this world and undermined the distorted idea that suffering cannot be beautiful. Jesus came to define the Kingdom of God. Jesus came to show what it means when the Lord reigns.

Suffering as redemptive is a hard, controversial message. The Alexamenos graffito is a drawing from a wall in Rome. Discovered in 1857, this image is considered the earliest known depiction (think graffiti) of Jesus' crucifixion, and it allows today's spiritual seeker to glimpse what a scandal it was to claim allegiance to a *crucified* leader. Refering to the man standing at the foot of the cross, the inscription reads, "Alexamenos worshipping his God."

The Alexamenos graffito, and a tracing to allow you to see the image more clearly. Both images are taken from *Ancient Rome in the Light of Recent Discoveries* by Rodolfo Lanciani.[2]

To worship a crucified Jesus was to worship an ass. In many philosophical constructs, ancient and modern, the crux of Christianity is the butt of the joke. But even before the crucifixion took place, Jesus had begun to teach his disciples that he would be rejected by the religious power brokers, would be killed by God's alleged leaders, and would over come their misguided murder by rising from the dead. He taught this bluntly, and when Peter protested, Jesus rebuked Peter and the notion that Jesus could not and would not suffer.

Then he called the crowd to him along with his disciples and said: "If anyone would come after me, he must deny himself and take up his cross and follow me. For whoever wants to save his life will lose it, but whoever loses his life for me and for the gospel will save it. What good is it for a man to gain the whole world, yet forfeit his soul? Or what can a man give in exchange for his soul? If anyone is ashamed of me and my words in this adulterous and sinful generation, the Son of Man will be ashamed of him when he comes in his Father's glory with the holy angels." (Mark 8:34–8, NIV)

Sally suffered.
We suffer. We cause others to suffer.
Bruised feet.
Yahweh Malach.
Jesus.
It is one thing to identify with the pain Jesus endured. Many in our world can identify with the pain of Jesus. Those who've been raped, mangled, and maligned due to war and oppression easily identify with the suffering of Jesus. One reason the Roman Catholic Church has exploded in Latin America over the last thirty years is the natural affinity that oppressed persons have for the Jesus who suffers and dies at the hands of dominating governments.

I have suffered very little in my life. I've never worried about where my next meal would come from. I've never stayed up at night because of violent nightmares. I do know shame, though. I know shame inti-mately. I've been a part of things that brought great shame, and I think about those events often. I know the feeling of deep-seated guilt and embarrassment for the fact that some of my life betrays the Christ-confession I made in baptism.

When I live in the Gospel of Mark and understand the shame of Jesus, this story becomes my story, for Jesus is not only taking on the shame of the first-century world, he's taking on the shame of all centu-ries, including the twenty-first. Jesus is not only embracing the shame of Peter, he's embracing the shame of Josh. I'm part of this story for life. This is the story that names, describes, and transforms my life as no other story can.

Jesus helps us re-imagine what "Yahweh Malach" means.

Slowly take in *these* words.

The soldiers led Jesus away into the palace [that is, the Praetorium] and called together the whole company of soldiers. They put a purple robe on him, then twisted together a crown of thorns and set it on him. And they began to call out to him, "Hail, king of the Jews!" Again and again they struck him on the head with a staff and spit on him. Falling on their knees, they paid homage to him. And when they had mocked him, they took off the purple robe and put his own clothes on him. Then they led him out to crucify him. (Mark 15:16–20, NIV)

As one views the ancient mockery of Jesus' crucifixion, one would be remiss in failing to realize the mockery we often make of Jesus' defi-nition of Kingdom when we try to define it by nationalism or pros-perity gospels or denominational doctrines we sometimes crown king instead of Jesus himself.

God reigns *in* our lives. For a Christian, that truth is more than can be captured in a single song or Bible verse. It's something that affects our lives in a profound way. It means that in times of hope and in time of despair, "the Kingdom of God is here."

The Christian story dares people to look at the world with different eyes—like looking at ugly feet and calling them beautiful. The Christian story dares each person to look at a man on a cross, to believe that he is God, and to believe that through him the kingdom of God has come near, that this story of a king who died on a cross two thousand years ago is a story that transforms lives today.

In Isaiah, God used a messenger, ugly feet and all, to proclaim, "Your God reigns." In the Gospel of Mark, we see Jesus as our messenger—ugly cross and all, ugly feet, ugly hands. And yet we say, "Beautiful."

The Christian story offers those who suffer a means of hope, for though pain is the result of a broken world, suffering is often the doorway to true and everlasting beauty—beauty that transcends time, culture, and geographic location. We must read the *whole* story.

The Gospel of Mark has a controversial ending. The most reliable early manuscripts and other ancient witnesses do not include Mark 16:9–20. I used to feel unsettled that the oft-quoted line, "Go into all the world and preach the good news to all creation," isn't actually in the most reliable manuscripts. It makes so much sense for it to be there. The problem is that many readers have never given the original ending a fair chance. Allow the drama of this ending to seep into your soul.

When the Sabbath was over, Mary Magdalene, Mary the mother of James, and Salome bought spices so that they might go to anoint Jesus' body. Very early on the first day of the week, just after sunrise, they were on their way to the tomb and they asked each other, "Who will roll the stone away from the entrance of the tomb?"

But when they looked up, they saw that the stone, which was very large, had been rolled away. As they entered the tomb, they saw a young man dressed in a white robe sitting on the right side, and they were alarmed.

"Don't be alarmed," he said. "You are looking for Jesus the Nazarene, who was crucified. He has risen! He is not here. See the place where they

laid him. But go, tell his disciples and Peter, 'He is going ahead of you into Galilee. There you will see him, just as he told you.'"

Trembling and bewildered, the women went out and fled from the tomb. They said nothing to anyone, because they were afraid. (NIV)

This is a dramatic ending. The gospel started with this dramatic messenger, John the Baptist, pointing toward the Lord. And the story ends with this angel pointing toward the Lord.[3]

People pointing. That's the definition of messengers. Like Isaiah's soldier messenger with ugly feet, like John the Baptist, like Mark the evangelist, like the angel in the tomb, like our ultimate messenger Jesus Christ, Christians go about their lives *pointing*. Pointing the world to an ugly scene of a death on a cross. A broken body. Blood running down. A crown of thorns and a sign that mocks the world's definition of "king." An ugly scene perhaps. Yet, we declare, "*Beautiful*." The Jesus Way reminds us that only God can turn suffering into beauty.

——

I was invited to sit on a panel at Michigan State University as a part of a program led by Christian leaders entitled "Join the Conversation"—a dialogue about faith and spirituality for people of all faiths.

Toward the end of a long night, in which we talked about theodicy, creation, evolution, theism, atheism, war, nonviolence, and ethics, one of the panelists ended the discussion with a story. This is my recollection.

When he was a boy, he remembered responding to the story of Jesus without realizing it. He was watching a dramatic production entitled "The Patsy" starring Sammy Davis, Jr. In the episode, Davis plays the lone minority in a regiment full of white soldiers. Davis is ridiculed, mocked, and despised. The soldiers tell him to go get striped paint, and Davis goes to fetch it. When he comes back he's jeered. They tell Davis to get a left-handed monkey wrench; Davis goes but has no luck securing one. He is the quintessential "patsy."

Toward the end of the story, the soldiers decide to play a mean trick on Davis. They take him out to the grenade field and hand him a grenade that is not operable. Davis, however, does not know this. One of the soldiers pulls the pin and all the soldiers who've gathered for the joke scatter like birds, leaving the young soldier all by himself.

They look back and see something they had no language for. Davis is lying prostrate on the ground using his body as a human shield while screaming, "Don't worry guys, I'll save you. I'll protect you. Run!"

"And that was my first real experience with the power of the gospel," said this follower of Jesus who was now sitting next to me almost fifty years later.[4]

We are taught to resist pain. We are instructed to avoid suffering. A deep spirituality molded in the image of Jesus takes root when we realize that God manages to use suffering to transform darkness, disillusionment, suffering, pain, and ugliness into everlasting beauty. The Psalmist claims, "In my distress I called to the Lord; . . . he rescued me from my powerful enemy . . . he brought me into a spacious place." The Apostle Paul proclaimed, "I want to know Christ and the power of his resurrection and the fellowship of sharing in his sufferings," because he understood that suffering is a means by which God changes the world from its insistence on violence, revenge, corruption, and domination.

The Gospels remind me that it is the risen Jesus full of hope and love who still bears the scars of his own crucifixion to prove the power of redemptive suffering. God turns what was once ugly into *lasting beauty.*[5]

Refugees become citizens.

Ugly feet become beautiful.

Patsys become life-changing heroes.

Crucified renegades emerge as the hope for the world.

This hope compels us to follow the risen renegade into God's big world.

PART TWO

LIVING REMINDERS

CHAPTER EIGHT

PROFESSOR JACK

*"The true atheist is the one who fails to see
the image of God in the least of these."*
—DOROTHY DAY

Jesus' teachings about risk, courage, injustice, suffering, and forgiveness have ushered me into some unexpected places. Like Cass
Corridor.

It's a notorious section of Detroit—known for rampant prostitu-
tion, drugs, and violence.[1] Those who live here lament, "The police
have given up on this place." The women and men who make this area
"home" have welcomed me with open arms; they invited me and my
friends into their space with love, acceptance, and genuine hospitality.

Cass Park Historic District is within a few stones' throw of mighty
Ford Field and Comerica Park, home to two professional sports teams:
the Detroit Tigers and Detroit Lions . . . okay, one and a half professional sports teams. These two super-sized stadiums, and the millions
of dollars they represent in profits each year, cast a long shadow over
this area the locals call "Jurassic Park," referring to the violence and
chaos often experienced by its inhabitants.

Some fellow Christians and I were involved in what we called a *love
feast*, trying to serve the people in Cass Corridor. Some of us already
had experience working with the poor, while others were experiencing

the power of "solidarity with the poor" (a concept Gustavo Gutierrez so aptly teaches us) for the first time. The *tsadiqim* decided to get together with the *anawim*.

During one of these love feasts, college students and lifelong disciples were working at a feverish and efficient pace. Quality dialog and community was breaking out all over this run-down property. One thing was obvious to me: my service was not needed. That's not as dire as it sounds. My wife and I decided that rather than being in the position of power that service can offer—a fallback position suburbanites often find more comfortable when working with the poor—we should seek out friends to talk with, to simply be present with.

My friend Andy Turner, who has taught me a great deal about city life, was already talking with several men at the southern end of the park. My wife and I joined him. I did not realize how meaningful these conversations would prove to be. None of my university or graduate training could match the education I was about to receive there.

Andy was talking with Jack, a homeless man who lived in a shelter near the park. I think of him as Professor Jack, which seems more appropriate, for he allowed the three of us into his classroom and offered us a humble but powerful lecture that could be titled "Life on the Margins." Jack's body was failing him, and he struggled to walk. Jack's mind, however, was as strong as ever.

Jack admitted he'd made a lot of poor decisions in his life. He'd been battling a drug addiction for some time, and he was on the streets because of it. But he also had had a good many decisions made for him, things that were beyond his control. This truth, articulated so nicely by Barbara Brown Taylor, struck me several times during our conversation: "Humans do not lose control. We lose the illusion that we were ever in control in the first place."

If you had the eyes to see and the ears to hear, it was quite the holy conversation. There were no pews, sacraments, or prayers—but God was closer to us than the blood in our veins. We took more church members and college students to sit in Professor Jack's classroom over the course of the next several weeks, but in that first session, my wife and I were taught a few things we will treasure for the rest of our lives. Here are a few of the things Professor Jack shared with his new pupils.

I made the mistake of saying that complaints from some who didn't care for the food were "no big deal."

"No, it is a big deal," said Jack. "They need to be grateful for what you've brought. We're human beings just like you. Don't say 'that's no big deal'—expect something from us just like you would *any other human*."

My definition of dignity was shallow in comparison with Jack's. One of the college students present in the park was smoking a cigarette, to which Jack replied, "I'm just glad there are still Christians who smoke." This line has become famous among those of us who welcomed Jack into our lives. Professor Jack taught us a great lesson about respect.

When I asked him what people could do for the poor and homeless, he replied, "Make us feel *real*. We want to feel like we are real people. You've done that today. See us. Talk to us. Be with us. Help us *feel*. It isn't just about feeding us or giving us clothes, it's about *seeing us*."

I have often prayed this simple prayer since sitting at Jack's feet:

God teach me how to see the divine image in every person I encounter. Let there be no invisible people in my life.

Professor Jack also taught us about politics. Referring to the many Catholic Churches in Detroit who've resisted white flight, he declared: "You think the city or any other government cares about the poor? You're crazy. The only thing holding things together for the homeless are the churches. If it wasn't for the churches, things would be unmentionable. I can't even imagine what would happen if the churches weren't invested in the city."

And in discussing the ambivalent attitudes of government toward the poor, he noted: "They [the local government] don't even have places for the poor to use the bathroom. We have to do the most self-degrading things just to use the bathrooms . . . makes us feel like animals. Know what I'm saying?" I wish I could've replied, "Yeah, Jack, I feel your pain." But if I did, I'd be lying. I did not know the pain pent up inside of Jack.

After I left this first meeting, Andy and Jack continued to talk about life, pain, and meaning. At one point, Jack pulled out a candy bar and offered it to Andy. "I couldn't," Andy reacted.

"Why not? C'mon, they won't let me take it back into the shelter. Have this with me. Share this with me."

"All right, thanks a lot, man."

Hearing Andy describe this moment, I thought that this was one of the best communion stories I'd heard in a long time. There was no bread or wine present, but the holy solidarity embodied by Christ was illuminating each passing second.

Before I left the park that serene autumn day in Detroit, I asked Professor Jack if there was anything that Kara and I could do for him. I looked him dead in the eye, making myself vulnerable to any request he might throw out there. "Tell me what you need, Jack."

He replied quickly and humbly, "I'm fine, really. I'm good. What you've done today, keep doing this."

It is difficult for persons who are used to being in the role of giver to be in the position of receiver. Until we follow this aspect of Jesus' message, moving from host to hosted, we will miss out on the true power of God's way in our lives. Professor Jack taught us about authentic community.

—〜〜—

I got a call ten days after Thanksgiving from Francis, one of Jack's friends in the shelter.

"Josh," Francis said, "it's not good."

"What's not good?"

"You don't know? It's Jack, man. He's dead. They rushed him out of here to Detroit Receiving. I know you were working with him, I know you were close. I just thought I'd call to tell you. Jack often talked about 'the priest,' that's you—I thought the right thing to do would be to call you."

"What do you mean he died? He just left me a message. We're supposed to have dinner soon."

"They suspect he overdosed, I'm not sure."

"Maybe he's still in the hospital? Francis, maybe he . . ."

"Josh, I'm telling you, man, this man is dead." I knew Francis was telling me the honest truth; I simply could not receive it. My plans for Jack were suddenly useless, pointless naïve notions to keep hope alive. Death did not fit any of those plans.

"Francis, you have no idea how much this phone call means to me."

Immediately, I went online, combing furiously through the death notices in the obituary section. After a few minutes, I found a notice for Jack on the website of the *Detroit News*:

IANNUCCI JOHN B. *December 05, 2006:* "JACK" Age 50, December 1, 2006. Loving father of Melissa Iannucci (Rich Thompson), Jacqueline, Lia, and Ezra. Cherished grandfather of Devin, Sydney, and Zoë. Dearest son of John (Yolanda) and the late Barbara. Brother of Patricia (Jon) Iannucci-Waller, Lea, Dino, Nancy (David) Welke and the late Frank. Uncle of Dylan, Alex, and Isabella. Former husband of Patty. Liz, mother of Jack's son Ezra. Funeral Wednesday Noon at the A.H. Peters Funeral Home, 20705 Mack Ave. at Vernier Rd., Grosse Pointe Woods. Visitation Tuesday 2-9 p.m. with a Rosary at 7 p.m. Memorials may be made to the Salvation Army, 16130 Northland Drive, Southfield, MI 48075.

All those names of children, parents, siblings, nieces and nephews. Jack was not merely a "junkie" or a "bum"—he was a man with an amazing story. He also played in a band, wrote poetry, owned a restaurant, loved his kids, and dabbled in academics at the local university.

I attended the viewing and funeral for John "Jack" Iannuchi (pronounced EYE-A-KNEW-CHEE). Jack's family and friends (whom I was meeting for the first time) huddled around my phone to listen to his voice. I saved a voicemail he left me the week prior to his death, wishing me a belated Happy Thanksgiving. We had been planning to have dinner together. "I'm really sorry I can't make it. I've just been feeling awful lately," rang Jack's now-savored message. His sisters and daughters had not heard his voice in quite some time due to the intervention process, which required tough love.

Jack's family, to my complete surprise, asked me to have a part in the funeral because Jack told them about the "priest he'd been working with." Never had I been so proud to be called "priest." (Though I was also thinking, "Did you clear this with the *real* priest?")

When I walked into the cathedral, I felt a lump in my throat. A young woman sang "Ave Maria" as Jack's body lay stiff and cold in the casket some twenty feet ahead of me at the end of the center aisle.

Just before the morning mass began, two men walked up to the front of the sanctuary toward Jack's body. One was a middle-aged white man. The other, a younger black man. They were both wearing their best, though their best would not fly in most of the churches I frequent.

Almost instantly, I recognized them.

Cass Park.

They lived in the Salvation Army Shelter I'd frequented in my visits to see Jack. One of the men placed his head on the dead body. He wept, for a leader and member of his community had been taken from him. "To watch over a man who grieves," one Jewish spiritualist writes, "is a more urgent duty than to think of God."[2]

I could barely find the right words during the funeral. I told his family, "Jack had a mind of great intellect. My undergraduate and graduate education in college was no match for his wisdom. More than a great mind, Jack had a huge heart. Very few people possess great knowledge and great love. Jack—your father, brother, husband, and grandfather—was such a person."

As I live, work, and play in Detroit and her suburbs, I often think about Jack and the rest of the homeless community in the inner city there: the truly marginalized and invisible people of my privileged world. I'm a better follower of Jesus for knowing Jack. Even more, I'm a better human being.

Now you know a little slice of Jack's story. Now, perhaps, you will taste differently words that have changed my life. When Jesus returns, in all of his splendor, accompanied by angels, he will separate all people of the world, past, present and future by how we lived:

> *"'I was hungry and you fed me,*
> *I was thirsty and you gave me a drink,*
> *I was homeless and you gave me a room,*
> *I was shivering and you gave me clothes,*
> *I was sick and you stopped to visit,*
> *I was in prison and you came to me.'*

"*Then those 'sheep' are going to say, 'Master, what are you talking about? When did we ever see you hungry and feed you, thirsty and give you a drink? And when did we ever see you sick or in prison and come to you?' Then the King will say, 'I'm telling the solemn truth: Whenever you did one of these things to someone overlooked or ignored, that was me—you did it to me.'*

"*Then he will turn to the 'goats,' the ones on his left, and say, 'Get out, worthless goats! You're good for nothing but the fires of hell. And why? Because—*

> *I was hungry and you gave me no meal,*
> *I was thirsty and you gave me no drink,*
> *I was homeless and you gave me no bed,*
> *I was shivering and you gave me no clothes,*
> *Sick and in prison, and you never visited.'*

"*Then those 'goats' are going to say, 'Master, what are you talking about? When did we ever see you hungry or thirsty or homeless or shivering or sick or in prison and didn't help?'*

"*He will answer them, 'I'm telling the solemn truth: Whenever you failed to do one of these things to someone who was being overlooked or ignored, that was me—you failed to do it to me."* (Matthew 25:34–45, The Message)

I'm not sure of the precise reason I am passionate about writing and speaking about Jack. I suppose it is therapeutic and healing for one thing. I recently had lunch with Francis, Jack's friend in the shelter, the one who first called me about Jack's death. Francis and I shared more stories about our mutual friend. Telling the stories of those who've gone before us is soothing for the soul.

I suppose I also write about Jack because I want suburbanites and those indifferent or calloused, regardless of religious orientation, to rethink the stereotypes that drive so much of our politics and attitudes regarding the marginalized people among us.

The main reason I write about Jack, though, might surprise you. Because of Jack, I am just beginning to understand who Jesus really was when he walked among us: jobless, homeless, penniless, rumored to be the illegitimate son of an illegitimate mother. Jack teaches me that the poor want to be known, for the poor, like the rich, have faces, names, histories, and stories. Perhaps this is the way God intended it to be: for us to get out of our holy ghettoes, out from behind our political posturing, and into the dangerous places of brokenness.[3]

CHAPTER NINE

A Place at the Table

"We are all intermeshed in an inescapable mutuality."
—Harry Emerson Fosdick

A few years ago, I found myself in a peculiar spot. My friend Francis and I had been having conversations about his possibly leaving the shelter where he was currently living, the shelter where Professor Jack overdosed. He was slowly becoming more and more receptive to my urgings.

After several conversations, I asked if I could take him out to dinner when he got off work. He agreed.

At that time, Francis was working at the ritziest mall in all of Metro Detroit. This mall is known, where I live, as the Sommerset Collection. Francis' work badge read "Janitor." I hope you sense, as I did, the odd juxtaposition of his home and his place of employment. Each morning, he rose from the shelter and rode a bus two hours to work. Because his shift lasted anywhere from four to eight hours, he regularly spent as much time on the bus as he did working. Public transportation in Detroit is notoriously slow and unreliable.

I knew Francis needed a friend and resource. As soon I as started having this thought, I knew it was God's way of saying, "Josh, that person is *you*. You have a nice salary, extensive education—for once, use what you've been blessed with *for someone else.*" (This is why I'm not a person who asks for God's voice to speak audibly into his life. I know my own experiences, and I've read the Bible. When God speaks, lives get messed up, turned upside down. God's whisper is earth-shattering enough for me.)

I picked Francis up at ten o'clock. We went to T. G. I. Friday's. On the way, he commented, "I've not been to a *real* restaurant in several years." Francis was only twenty-nine, a young man with almost two years of college experience, a 3.7 G.P.A. In the ensuing weeks, Francis and I would talk about the Iraq War, immigration, suffering, love, and, of course, the Detroit Pistons.

At the restaurant, I recommended three options. First option: Francis could do nothing. He could continue to spin his wheels in the mud and stay content with getting by. Second option: Francis could begin looking for a different job, one that paid full-time. But even in this plan he needed to get out of the shelter within a few months. Or the third option: Francis could move into my home for a determined period of time, with the idea of enrolling in South Oakland Shelter, going back to school, and getting a full-time job. In all three scenarios, my wife and I agreed to help Francis by any means necessary, including substantial financial support.

Francis chose the option I would have chosen: option three. That night, to my surprise, Francis agreed to gather all of his possessions, which were being stored in a room at the shelter, and come stay with the Graves family for the week.

I vividly remember waiting in the parking lot of the Salvation Army Shelter in Cass Park that cold December day in Downtown Detroit. I heard suburbanites of old who whispered, "Stay away from Cass Park. I don't care what time of day. That's bad news." I heard the voices of my homeless friends who lived in the area who were fond of referring to Cass Park as "Jurassic Park" or "Crack Park." I also recalled the words of one police officer: "Pound for pound, Cass Park is one of the worst areas in the United States."

I couldn't go inside, since the shelter allows only residents inside after ten o'clock. While waiting outside, I witnessed two men smoking a crack pipe on the sidewalk beside me. I saw one older woman trying to turn a trick. I remember thinking, "*I* would mug me right now."

Here I am, a young white guy from the 'burbs, and I was afraid.

But then I thought to myself, *If I died at midnight in Cass Park trying to help a homeless man, I'd be a hero in some circles. This isn't a bad way to die. This is great! No one would know I was afraid. They'd simply hold me up as the champion of bringing the rich and poor together.* That is, I remembered, unless the autopsy report revealed soiled pants and an ultra high blood pressure at the time of death, or worse . . . as the *cause* of death. Yeah; I was afraid.

After a few awkward conversations with men who lived on the streets in the area, Francis finally gathered all of his stuff and was ready to go. He stayed with us that night and claimed the next morning, "I slept better than I have slept in a long, long time."

Francis enrolled in a temporary shelter and now lives in his own place in the city, working a full-time job. When I've shared this story with some people in the past, they've responded automatically by saying, "I can't believe you allowed a homeless man to stay in your house." But Kara and I weren't letting a "homeless man" stay with us. We were allowing *our friend*, Francis Kibarra, to sleep in a bed we seldom used.

When the word hospitality pokes its head in casual conversation, people usually think of one of two things: what I do for my family; or what I do for my friends. But drawing on his training in Torah,[1] Jesus taught that hospitality is much more countercultural: hospitality is about welcoming those who do not have a family or friends:

Then Jesus said to his host, "When you give a luncheon or dinner, do not invite your friends, your brothers or relatives, or your rich neighbors; if you do, they may invite you back and so you will be repaid. But when you give a banquet, invite the poor, the crippled, the lame, the blind, and you will be blessed. Although they cannot repay you, you will be repaid at the resurrection of the righteous." (Luke 14:12–14, The Message)

Jesus seems downright dogmatic that, in his economy, everybody is a *somebody*.

One test of fidelity to God's kingdom is to consider the people in whom you are invested who cannot tangibly pay you back. Or, to use another economic metaphor, are you in relationship with people who have nothing to offer you in return?

Christian ethics do not involve merely figuring out the rules or creating a new kind of moralism. Rather, the Christian ethic is living God's future on display in the present. When the Scriptures talk about a day when every tongue will confess and every knee will bow, when swords will be used for stewardship and not death, when the lion and the lamb will have a play date together, when skin color and gender and politics will no longer define and divide us—this is what it means to live God's future in the present world. We're called to bring this vision into the now.

Reclaiming Christian hospitality is a vital step for the church in this emerging world we all find ourselves in. Jerome, an early father of the church, once wrote, "Let poor men and strangers be guests at your table and with them Christ shall be your guest." Hospitality is not merely helping out our fellow man; hospitality ushers in the presence of God into one's life.[2]

I frequently ask myself and fellow Christians this question: "What might it mean to practice radical hospitality in this confusing world we live in?" I am going to borrow from Christine Pohl and suggest that the Church must learn to be converted to two essential teachings of the New Testament: First, the Church must universalize whom we deem to be a "neighbor." Second, the Church must learn to "welcome all strangers."[3]

I mean "universalize our definition of neighbor" the way Jesus taught in the Gospel of Luke, chapter 10. The parable commonly known as the Good Samaritan is found in only this one Gospel. A lawyer, seeking to put Jesus to the test, asks Jesus, "What must I do to inherit eternal life?" Today, we would say, "Pastor, how do I get to heaven?" Jesus asks this expert in the law, "What is written in the Law?" Don't you hate it when you ask someone a question and instead of answering it, they ask another question? Good teachers do that— they lead their students to figure it out themselves. A good teacher is more interested in teaching you *how* to think than *what* to think.

The lawyer, because this is his bag, gives the right answer. Doing his homework out of Deuteronomy 6:4–9 and related passages, commonly referred to as the *Shema* (which literally means, "listen up!"), he answers, "You shall love the Lord your God with all your heart, and with all your soul, and with your strength, and with all your mind." But he does not stop there. He's been paying attention to the Jesus Way. "And . . . love your neighbor as yourself." Like a schoolteacher, Jesus puts a sticker on the lawyer's participation chart, "You have provided the right answer; do this and you will go to heaven."

This would be a good story in itself: Lawyer wants to test Jesus. Jesus, instead, puts lawyer to test. Lawyer gives right answer. Everyone goes home a winner.

But the lawyer is not content to stop there; he wants to "justify himself." He asks Jesus another question: "Who is my neighbor?" And Jesus tells the man, and everyone else in the crowd, a story:

A man was going down from Jerusalem to Jericho, when he fell into the hands of robbers. They stripped him of his clothes, beat him and went away, leaving him half dead. A priest happened to be going down the same road, and when he saw the man, he passed by on the other side. So too, a Levite, when he came to the place and saw him, passed by on the other side. But a Samaritan, as he traveled, came where the man was; and when he saw him, he took pity on him. He went to him and bandaged his wounds, pouring on oil and wine. Then he put the man on his own donkey, took him to an inn and took care of him. The next day he took out two silver coins and, gave them to the innkeeper. "Look after him," he said, "And when I return, I will reimburse you for any extra expense you may have." (Luke 10:30–5, NIV)

Some who study this story say that the priest and the Levite are in a bind. They are men of God, but the law of God binds them from helping lest they become "unclean" by touching a dead body. Corpses, in this interpretive framework, are as incongruous as a preacher going to Vegas on Christmas—they just don't go together. Out of this understanding, some believe that Jesus is challenging their love of keeping the law versus their love of people.

Others who study this story say that the Samaritan in the story represents the minority person in any given culture. The priest becomes the "conservative Christian" and the Samaritan becomes the "gay man some love to hate." Or the Levite represents the "rich" and the Samaritan is the "homeless woman in Cass Park." Or, the Levite represents "angry citizens" and the Samaritan is the "illegal resident among us." While all of these are challenging social constructs to consider, I don't think they finally get at what is going on in the story.

Something deeper is going on in this story. One Jewish thinker has opened up this parable in drastic ways for me. She writes,

> To understand this parable in theological terms, we need to see the image of God in everyone, not just members of our own group. To hear this parable in contemporary terms, we should think of ourselves as the person in the ditch and then ask, "Is there anyone from any group, about whom we'd rather die than acknowledge, *She offered help* or *He showed compassion*?" More, is there any group whose members might rather die than help us? If so, then we find the modern equivalent for the Samaritan.[4]

"Those people," "redneck," "white-trash," "towel head," "you *know* how Mexicans are," "white people are mean," "I just don't get the mentality in Detroit"—such sentiments have no place in the vocabulary of a Christian. The Good Samaritan may wish to converse with us on this matter.

> Good Samaritan: "May I come in?"
>
> Josh: "Certainly."
>
> Good Samaritan: "I won't stay long. I have a story I want to tell."
>
> Josh: "By all means. You're in the Bible; who am I to stop you?"
>
> Good Samaritan: "A man was traveling in the West Bank . . . you know. . . Ancient Samaria. A Jewish man is beat up and left for dead on the side of the road. A rabbi walks by, sees his fellow Jew, and keeps going. A rabbi in training walks by, some time later, sees his fellow Jew, and also passes by. Then, after some time a member of Al Qaeda walks down the same path . . ."
>
> Josh: "Al Qaeda . . . what?"
>
> Good Samaritan: "Let me finish. This man, belonging to Al Qaeda, does what the Jewish leaders won't. This man sees the beaten man as a man worthy of his time. Josh, I ask you a question. Which man was being a neighbor? The point, after all these years is not who is your neighbor? The point is for all who read the Gospels to realize that in Jesus' teaching and life, everyone is a neighbor. There's no one who's not your neighbor. Now maybe you see why some wanted to kill Jesus because he taught like he did and told stories like this one?"

The Good Samaritan story is ultimately interested in how *we* see those around us. It is not an accident, for instance, that immediately preceding the Good Samaritan parable, Jesus made this statement to his disciples: "Blessed are the eyes that *see* what you *see*. For I tell you that many prophets and kings wanted to see what you see but did not see it, and to hear what you hear but did not hear it."[5]

I've experienced Jesus' radical definition of "neighbor" in my own life. September 11 shook us all up. But no longer do I see the woman at the bank with an Arab name as an enemy. No longer do I see the man on the plane with a turban as an enemy. No longer do I suspect the Muslim I grew up with of being an enemy. In the world imagined by Jesus, *everyone* is my neighbor.[6]

One Christian drives this point home in a moment of unforeseen opportunity. Shane Claiborne decided to serve as an agent of reconciliation in Iraq as the most recent war first unfolded.[7] He traveled to Iraq to serve those who were innocent victims of war. While in transit, Claiborne found himself sitting between two men who had much in common with each other, including their political convictions. The men cracked jokes regarding "liberals" and proceeded to boast about America's military presence in Iraq. Instead of engaging in a heated debate, Claiborne attempted an unusual tactic. He unveiled some homemade cookies, offering a bit of solidarity with his row-mates. The men asked, "Where are you headed?" Claiborne got a lump in his throat.

"Baghdad." His acquaintances were in shock.

"Are you in the military?" asked one of the puzzled men. Claiborne laughed, knowing that he did not fit the stereotype, with his dreadlocks and all. "No," he said, "I will be going as a Christian peacemaker to be with the families there and voice opposition to the war." Having the benefit of time and space, Claiborne later reflected on the significance of this encounter:

> I was amazed to see that they did not start arguing with me.
> They were intrigued that I believed in something so much that
> I would risk my life for it. We actually had a nice talk. And I
> will never forget what they said as we parted. These two people
> whom I had just met told me with great drama how "glued"
> they would be to the T.V. as they worried about me, wonder-
> ing if I would make it back safely. I stood in awe, knowing that
> the great tragedy is that we have no face to war. Degrees of

separation allow us to destroy human beings we do not know except as *enemy*, as if Iraq was filled with millions of Saddams or Osamas, and no children. In one hour, the walls came down a little. I thought of how powerful it was to have a face in Iraq, albeit a face these two had only met for a couple of hours on a plane. But now they hesitate as they hear the drums of war. And in the moment of hesitation, Truth is birthed. Granted, I would like for my two new friends to oppose the war because of the families in Iraq, but if they oppose the war because of some goofball they met for an hour on a plane, that'll work for now.[8]

If we learn to universalize who we define as neighbor, we then must begin to welcome *strangers among us*. Of course, the New Testament has something to say about this.

Eat this text.

"Keep on loving each other as brothers. Do not forget to entertain strangers, for by so doing some people have entertained angels without knowing it. Remember those in prison as if you were their fellow prisoners, and those who are mistreated as if you yourselves were suffering." (Hebrews 13:1–3)

Two stories from my own life come to mind immediately.

The first story stars a homeless friend of mine, Jamaican Frank.

Christ Church Macomb (CC:M, the first multi-site effort for the church I served) launched in 2008. That first Sunday was a day to remember for many reasons. I had been planning to spend all week in Cass Park with several students from Rochester College for an *Urban Plunge*. This is an annual urban spiritual formation retreat, one of the highlights of the year for me. Because we were coming from Cass Park, where we'd just fed almost three hundred people, I decided to invite a few of my homeless friends to the opening worship gathering of Christ Church, which was meeting in an elementary school. I thought they would enjoy the experience, and I thought it would be good for the folks present at the launch.

About halfway through the time of worship, a friend tapped on my shoulder.

"They need you in the men's bathroom right away."

"What's wrong?" I asked.

"They need you now."

I told my wife, "I'll be right back."

As I approached the bathroom, some of the students explained to me what happened. One of our friends from Cass Park decided to make the most of the excellent facilities. Frank, an older man with a deep Caribbean accent almost impossible to interpret, was now standing mostly naked (work with me here) in the bathroom, in front of the sink, giving himself a makeshift bath.

Later, my lifelong friend Ashley Harrison would report the reaction of the school janitor (who talks exactly like Joe Pesci). "Ashley . . . this can't happen. He's *naked.*"

Ashley handled the situation like a champ.

Eventually we got Frank dressed, disaster averted. A few days later I emailed the leadership team of CC:M with a simple one-line response: "Team: CCM's tagline all year has been 'Come as you are' . . . I suppose Frank really believed this." If Frank showed up today, we'd make room for him. There's always room in this family.

The second story features Nic Paradise, who was an official member of our church community. An excellent artist and skater, Nic could not shake a drug addiction that had haunted him since he was a young teenager.

One particular Monday morning I received phone calls and texts from friends saying I "must" come to the apartment of a few young adults who were a part of our church. I knew something was wrong, but I never dreamed what I was about to walk into.

I pulled up to the apartments around ten A.M. The police had just arrived, along with a few family members. I walked into the apartment to find Nic, who was nineteen years old, overdosed on a combination of drugs. His body lay lifeless on the bed in the main bedroom. His body had begun to turn a shade of green I'd never before seen.

"He's been dead for some time," I heard someone whisper in a corner.

As I looked at his still body, I thought to myself, "This young man worshipped with us yesterday. He broke bread with us yesterday. He listened to me preach yesterday. The entire gathering prayed over him yesterday. He repeated a confession from *The Book of Common Prayer* with his other brothers and sisters in Christ . . . *yesterday*. And *today* . . . he's dead."

When Nic first came to our community of faith, he was an "other." He did not fit the normal demographic; he was a young skater with a flare for the dramatic. But he came into our community, and we loved him. We decided to cancel our normal worship service scheduled that week. Instead, we invited all of Nic's family and friends, most of whom have little interest in Christianity, to celebrate and mourn the loss of their brother, son, friend, and skater.

The sixty-minute worship and prayer gathering was a rare moment of hope and possibility in the rather dark season that proceeded. Liz Trainor was Nic's fiancée, and the two of them had a son together: Carter, a beautiful and healthy boy. Liz stood up with her close friend Shaun Hover and offered some simple but powerful words about Nic's infectious ability to draw people to himself. Several of Nic's peers were on hand to honor the bond and love shared by classmates and skate-partner friends spanning several years. During the time of remembrance, we played a video of Nic's greatest skateboarding moments. Many of Nic's friends present were skateboarders themselves. I think they appreciated seeing Nic in his primary element; the place where his rather chaotic life most made sense. As a former athlete, I admired the courage and athleticism required for skateboarding.

Welcoming one stranger allowed our church to welcome a host of strangers. Even as I write, I can hear the voices of these new friends adding, "Yeah, you were strangers *to us*."

I'm not a prophet or a son of a prophet, but I'm willing to guess most of the group present on behalf of Nic had not stepped foot in a church building in quite some time. Some, perhaps, were there for the very first time. Our church liked to say that we existed to "connect all people to Jesus." This was a great thing to write on a piece of paper or post on a website as a mission statement. But it's a difficult project. It isn't for the faint of heart. It isn't sexy. It certainly isn't the most comfortable way to be the church. We tried to follow Jesus to the dangerous places. The places everyone else ran from were the places we believed God was calling us to run toward. If others ran from the projects, from the homeless, from single moms, from skateboarders with drug problems—we ran to them.

In the months following Nic's death, several people began coming in and out of our faith community. Shaun Hover is now a missionary, training other young adults, including skaters, to practice hospitality all over the world.

Another young man, like Nic, struggled with a heroine addiction. Once when he and I approached the Eucharist together at the front of the church gathering, he grabbed the plastic cup of wine, mashing it against my cup and saying, "Cheers to the way of Jesus." I couldn't help but think that Jesus was in our midst, smiling in light of the motley crew he welcomed to his table; a table full of sinners, tax collectors, addicts, cowards—people who'd made a mess of their lives.

—⟶⟵—

Important as it is to welcome strangers, it is equally important to learn the art of *being* welcomed. That's what Professor Jack taught me. That's also what Anne Harvey taught me.

I first met Anne outside a building near Cass Park called "The Dog Pound." The building, housing some fifty family units, got its endearing name for two reasons. First, I'm told, the man who owns the building keeps dogs in the basement, so dogs bark and howl at all hours of the night. Second, the residents who live in this low-income building say they feel as if they live in a kennel.

The first time I met Anne was in February—the dead of a Michigan winter. I noticed Anne right away because she wore a summer dress with no shoes. *In the middle of winter. Twenty degrees outside. She has no shoes*, I thought to myself.

A few of us paid attention to Anne over the next several months— nothing spectacular, just little works of love to let her know she was valued. But then, from my experience, transformation usually happens "one phone call, twenty dollar check, home cooked casserole" at a time.

On a perfect day in October, while hosting a love feast in Cass Park, my cell phone rang. It was Anne.

"You gonna come get me?"

"What do you mean? Who is this?"

"This is Anne. You got to come get me. I'm in my new house."

I couldn't believe it. Anne was no longer living in The Dog Pound. She'd gotten back on her feet, rented a house in a better part of the city, regained custody of her kids. "I want you to come get me and bring me back to Cass Park so I can tell everyone about my new place. I want to have a party."

When I picked Anne up some thirty minutes later, she was as proud as a young child hosting her first lemonade stand, as proud as a college graduate. Her smile exceeded her physical face.

"See my house," she said.

"I see your house, Anne. I'm proud of you."

So we planned to have a party at Anne's house. Once again, a bunch of *tsadiqim* and *anawim* getting together under the liberating name of Jesus. But before we had an opportunity to party in Anne's new digs, she left us tragically, dying from complications with diabetes. I've taken solace in the notion that Anne was likely going to die, whether or not our lives intersected her life. But for a few moments in time, we were able to help Anne see herself as God sees her: beautiful, beloved, cherished, and welcomed. Our friendship produced life, joy, and, most importantly, hope in the midst of great struggle. This is why I'm so attracted to the Jesus Way. In Jesus' economy, everyone has a place at the table. Everyone's invited; we don't get to check over the guest list for approval.

It's not our party.

CHAPTER TEN

FOOD AND WATER

*"If you give no thought (or worse, don't care) about the broken
body of the Master when you eat and drink, you're running
the risk of serious consequences. That's why so many of you
even now are listless and sick, and others have gone to an
early grave. If we get this straight now, we won't have to be
straightened out later on. Better to be confronted by the Master
now than to face a fiery confrontation later."*

—St. Paul in 1 Corinthians 11:29–32, The Message

*"That's what baptism into the life of Jesus means. When we are
lowered into the water, it is like the burial of Jesus; when we are
raised up out of the water, it is like the resurrection of Jesus. Each
of us is raised into a light-filled world by our Father so that we
can see where we're going in our new grace-sovereign country."*

—St. Paul in Romans 6:3–4, The Message

Every church has its peculiar practices and idiosyncrasies. My
particular tribe is, unfortunately, no exception. For me, Holy
Communion (the Lord's Supper or Eucharist, depending upon your
tribal language) conjures up two concrete images in my mind: white
suits and secret service men.

In my Christian tradition it goes something like this. Midway
through the worship service, there's a dramatic pause and all of a
sudden a platoon of men, usually dressed slightly better than they'd

dress on other days, stand and march to the proper position in the sanctuary.

If you're a visitor to this kind of thing, it might feel like the first time you go to the opera—you smile, nod your head, but inside you're thinking, "I'm not quite sure what's going on here." If you're in a conservative church, the designated men march to the front. If you're in a progressive church, the covert agents (maybe even women, depending on how progressive) march to the back—a stealth communion platoon of sorts.

As a young boy, I could imagine that the men in the congregation were training to be secret servicemen, hence: abrupt movement, stealth approach, suits and ties, proper posture (both hands folded in front), and clockwork precision. These men had to be in the secret service, I reasoned. How else did they know the exact moment to stand and secure their strategic location? I was quite sure they were all wearing listening devices with senior agents running the communion operations from an undisclosed location.

This is why I also think of white suits.

One Sunday, the secret servicemen of the church, plus my Dad (he was the only one I could be certain was *not* in covert ops since, at the time, he worked at Children's Hospital of Detroit and spent his other time with my brother and me), strategically positioned themselves in the front of the sanctuary. Standing next to my dad in the lineup was the man who we can call The Colonel—because, without fail, he wore a white suit when it was his rotation to serve in the mysterious band of brothers.

When my dad gets nervous, his hands sweat. This is a trait he regretfully passed on to at least one of his sons. You might see where this story is going. My father, bless his heart, received the tray in proper fashion: as a track star grasping the baton. The problem came not in the reception but in the passing.

The audience expectations for communion servers may not compare to what Olympic athletes feel, but the level of difficulty in passing the communion trays rivals the passing of the baton. As The Colonel handed the tray to my father, something went wrong. The purple juice resting in plastic cups drenched The Colonel's white suit. It was ugly.

My eyes bugged out, I sat up in my seat. My twin brother sat next to me as these dramatic events unfolded, and we wanted to laugh more than we wanted to breathe. We knew better though. We knew the secret servicemen might catch us and take us to a prison work camp in Siberia. And, for the most part, we actually liked living in Metro Detroit. I'm pretty sure my dad paid the dry cleaning bill for The Colonel. I don't remember that detail. I do remember, however, the intense desire to laugh, and, like a dam containing hundreds of gallons of water, my church upbringing holding me back.

One ministry colleague reports a time in his childhood church where the juice was passed on one side and the bread passed on the other. Eventually the two forces met in the middle of the congregation, putting the "passers" in an awkward dilemma. Their solution: the leaders went around asking, "Did you get bread or juice?" It was hardly the flawless orchestration they wanted, and in the end, the leaders of the church were so distressed, they invited the entire church body to come back for Sunday night services to "retake" the Lord's Supper.

As important as the practice of the Lord's Supper might be, we easily fall into the trap of self-deception and self-importance, forgetting that even in our faith, it is possible to take ourselves too seriously. Yet over time, Communion moments both silly and profound changed me in gospel ways.

—⁓—

I've grown to *need* the Lord's Supper each week. I can't live without it. Believe me, I've tried.

The Eucharist has become, for me, more a *meal* than a snack; a time not so much where I guilt my way into participation as much as a time to ask, "Where is God calling me to become more? Where is God calling me to live more into his mission for my life?" Some in traditions like mine, where we practice Communion each Sunday, are asking, "Do we lose appreciation for the supper by taking it every week? Should we take it less?" I usually respond, "No, we should take it more often." I'd like to see us engage in Communion during corporate worship, in small groups, and in the significant moments of our life. When I live in the story of Acts, which tells of the early believers' constancy in sharing Communion together,[1] I'm prompted to ask, "Why am I not practicing the holy meal more often?"

I love Sara Miles' description of the significance the holy meal has had in her spiritual journey. A former agnostic, Miles describes the Lord's Supper as the place where the esoteric, ethereal, and abstract notions of Christian belief are defeated by the truth that Christianity has always been a religion based upon tangible practices. Describing her first Communion, she writes, "Faith turned out not to be abstract at all, but material and physical. I'd thought Christianity meant angels and trinities and being good. Instead, I discovered a religion rooted in the most ordinary yet subversive practice: a dinner table where everyone is welcome, where the despised and outcast are honored."[2]

There's food and there's *food*.

When people gather to eat Jesus' meal, they are making a political and social statement. Following Jesus' example, Christians are turning the world upside down one table at a time. Every time we participate in Christ's meal, we are rehearsing a life of hospitality. This meal is the shape of God's grace. God is the host. It's his table. "So we take it and we taste," Rob Bell and Don Golden write. "We take part in this two-thousand-year-old ritual. . . . We 'do this' in all sorts of ways and in all sorts of places with all sorts of diversity. Some of us 'do this' with chants, and some of us in silence. In some settings people serve each other, and in other gatherings people serve themselves . . . . It changes us. It humbles us. It brings us together."[3]

The Lord's Supper is not the only practice that gives me material proof of God's grace in my life. Baptism has also resurrected my imagination. It is as meaningful a practice as there is in Christianity. There is power in this concrete public declaration. The moment in which I told the community of faith "I believe that Jesus Christ is God's only son" isn't tied to a moment in time but lives on forever, following me wherever I am. If my word and actions do not match my baptism, then I speak and live a word that does not belong to me.

Because I have been baptized, I am no longer an individual living my life for myself, for I now belong to something much more important than my accomplishments or failures—I'm being swept up in the work of God in the world. I no longer see the world through my own eyes but through the eyes of God's community. My life isn't nearly as important as the life of the church. "It's not that I think less of myself . . . it's that I think of myself *less* often," Anne Lamott reminds us. In this act, an old proverb is proven wrong. In this act, we see that actually, water can be thicker than blood.

Essentially, baptism is a physical act connected to a spiritual reality: God must first kill us before he can make us into the person he wants us to be. Upon witnessing a baptism at my church, one seeker noted, "Man, you have to really trust the person baptizing you. I mean, I won't just let anybody drown me under water." In a still more chilling version of baptism, I'm told by some friends from Uganda that, on occasion, when their churches are unable to locate running water, spiritual leaders dig life-size, grave-like holes and fill them with water: men and women find new life by being lowered into a watery grave. I find that image helpful. God must bury us before he can raise us to a different kind of life.[4]

For me, there was a mystery in the moment. Nothing seemed to change, yet I knew things were changed, something I could not even begin to explain. Somehow, I felt as if God himself reached down and washed away my sins. I am not the man I should be but thank God I'm not the man I used to be. Salvation might be a journey, but there are moments along the path that cannot be duplicated. For instance, a marriage is full of important events, but nothing can replace the actual wedding day—there is no substitute.

Baptism is a means to an end, and not the end itself. Ultimately, baptism is about being an apprentice of Jesus. We could have stayed among the crowds admiring, rooting, and yes, even worshiping Jesus. But in baptism, we step out of the crowd, get behind Jesus and say, "I'll follow you, whatever the cost." My baptism reminds me that God drenches me in his limitless grace each and every day. That one act is permanent, pointing constantly to Jesus' power to cleanse the dark parts of my soul.

There's water and there's *water*.

One important practice in the Christian life becomes the discipline of repeatedly telling our baptism stories. We tell these stories to our children, friends, and family. We tell these stories to anyone who will listen because these are the stories that define our lives, giving us a new identity. We tell the serious and the funny stories alike. We tell the mundane as well as the extraordinary. Recalling *all* of God's movement in our lives reminds us that God is interested in rescuing everyone from themselves. One such baptism retelling has stayed with me over the years.

My friend Patrick recalls an unusual baptism when he was ministering to a military church in Norfolk, Virginia. At this time, Patrick was considerably conservative in this theology and practice.

Two young sailors approached my friend with another sailor between them. They introduced Antonio, an Italian boy who'd joined the U.S. Navy so he could become an American citizen much faster. These two comrades were kind to Antonio when everyone else ragged him, messed with his bunk and gear—normal practice in military life. Their generosity made the young Italian want to know the "why" behind their actions. When his fellow soldiers told him about Jesus, they had his full attention.

The trio sought the minister out during a Sunday morning worship gathering. Antonio bear-hugged the minister and announced, "I'm a gonna' be baptized!" My friend assured Antonio that they could make time to engage in a discussion about that.

Patrick stood up to preach, and Antonio came and stood in front of the pulpit. Being a conservative traditionalist, Patrick went for it. He shortened the sermon somewhat since Antonio was standing three feet away, staring at him like a puppy in search of a home.

Patrick offered the invitation. Antonio was already there.

When Patrick asked Antonio if he knew what he was doing, Antonio responded, "Yes! I'm a gonna' be a baptized!" As Patrick prepared to take Antonio's confession of faith, Antonio sprinted for the door leading to the baptistery. Apparently, Antonio didn't have time for all of Patrick's formalities. "Once he heard that we were to go through that door, he went. I grabbed onto him and tried to drag him to a stop while asking him if he believed. . . . I wasn't entirely success-ful so we assumed that dragging a hefty preacher against his will was sufficient evidence of faith," Patrick would later relay to me.

When Patrick informed Antonio of the proper attire he was expected to wear, Antonio responded with incredulity. Patrick explained (rather brilliantly) that his old clothes were the clothes of iniquity and he was supposed to now wear the clothes of purity. So Antonio gave in, changed outfits, and headed straight for the baptis-try. Before Patrick could change his clothes, he saw Antonio running for the water.

"Wait," the befuddled preacher yelled.

"Why?"

Patrick describes this moment further:

In the tank I turned to him and found him in the pike posi-tion ready to dive in headfirst. I waved him off and physically held him, keeping him from plunging under; the whole time I pulled him down the stairs. While I tried to say my bit (I had a bit to say. I'm a preacher. That's what we do) he lifted his legs so that he could slide out of my arms and under the water. I restrained him. Frustrated with me keeping him from meeting Jesus in the water he put a leg up against the side of the tank

and shoved. We both went under. I barely got out 'in the name
of the Father, Son and Holy Spirit!' before I was submerged."

The force of the two men entering the water caused much of the water
in the baptistry to cascade onto the sacred table holding the bread and
wine of the Lord's Supper.[5]

Antonio had only been a Christian for two seconds and already he
was in trouble for messing with the sacred meal.

We remember and recount stories like this because they remind
us that God seems interested in working within our quirky characteristics and personality traits. The things that makes us "us" are the very
ingredients God uses to establish the holy amidst the mundane. These
practices give us the energy to continue our mission.

Baptism is a staple in the life of many contemporary churches,
which is nothing new. Baptism has been a part of the church's identity
since her inception. Baptism and the Lord's Supper are the two practices that have unequivocally stood the test of time.

Eat these words from Paul:

*That's what baptism into the life of Jesus means. When we are lowered
into the water, it is like the burial of Jesus; when we are raised up out of
the water, it is like the resurrection of Jesus. Each of us is raised into a
light-filled world by our Father so that we can see where we're going in
our new grace-sovereign country.* (Romans 6:1–23, The Message)

Consider the historical context into which Paul writes. Claudius,
the emperor of Rome, expelled all Jews in 49 A.D. Five years later, there's
a new sheriff, or emperor, in town. His name is Nero. You've probably
heard about him. In 54 A.D., Nero allows all Jews back into Rome. Jews
who both did and did not believe that Jesus was the Messiah.

Those people who comprised the Christian Church in Rome were
a mixture of Jewish and Roman Christians. Paul writes a letter to a
church that is trying to figure out both how to exist with members of

the family coming from the disparate perspectives of Jew and Gentile and how Roman Christians should react to those Jews who, whether or not they claim to follow Jesus, see the Roman Christians as impostors because they do not circumcise, keep Sabbath, or keep kosher. Paul sticks his hands into the messiness of this situation and constructs a letter to the entire church, both Jews and Romans, to address their two-front war.

Thus Romans, which many know as Paul's great treatise, was actually a pastoral letter written to specific people and circumstances. Perhaps the letter's enduring power should remind us that the most influential and effective writing and teaching comes out of real human drama, not the cozy confines of a library or office. The passage quoted above, from Romans, is pivotal because it reminds the reader that sin is a real power, a force to be reckoned with. But God, in his infinite wisdom and mercy, has provided the means by which all Christians—Jewish, Roman, American, Iranian—receive the Spirit of God, which enables us to continue the journey of becoming like Christ. Paul reminds his readers that they have been brought to the church through *the same baptism.*

The Lord's Supper and baptism are powerful lights for us, yet still we sometimes lose our way. I can feel the frustration of many believers. Intellectually, we *know* we are saved, a new creation. But to be honest, we don't feel like that all the time. We feel pretty average, not that different from those around us. If the Holy Spirit is alive and working in me, why do I continue to stumble, unable to let go of sin's hold on my life?

The two practices of the Lord's Supper and baptism are sometimes referred to as sacraments. This word conjures all kinds of meaning for some—sacred, distancing. Simply understood, though, sacraments are the physical manifestations of God's grace in our daily lives, visible things we do that partake of invisible realities. Sacraments are a connection between us and the divine in our midst. The food and water found within the two practices of communion and baptism are central in the Jesus Feast for they remind us of who we already are. The sacramental elements of our lives are the moments when the physical and spiritual mesh in unusual, holy ways.

Nicholas Sparks, a well-known novelist who's dealt with adversity his entire life, has cowritten a memoir with his brother Micah entitled *Three Weeks with My Brother*. This work is a story of tragedy and brokenness, mixed with redemption and healing. The adversity Sparks shares about his life fuels much of his writing on death, spirituality, relationships, disillusionment, and pain. Among other things, in the memoir, Sparks discusses the frustration he has shared with his wife in raising their son, Ryan, who suffers from a mild form of autism.

Reading Sparks' words made me think of two things. First, people with handicaps often resemble the heart of Jesus more than the allegedly "normal" people. Second, the relationship between parents and a handicapped child is a fair parallel to the relationship between God and his church. At one point, Sparks recalls:

> "Look," she finally ground out, "I know your year has been hard. But do you want to know what my year has been like?" She paused to draw a ragged breath. "I wake up every morning and I think about Ryan. And I look at my beautiful child, a child that I love more than life itself, and I wonder if he'll ever talk, or go to school, or play like the other kids. I wonder if he'll ever have a date, or drive a car, or go to the prom. I wonder if he'll ever get married. And I spend all day driving from doctor to doctor, and no one can tell us what's wrong, and no one can tell us what to do. He'll be four years old in a little while and I don't even know if he loves me. I think about this when I wake up, I think about this all day long, and it's the last thing I think about before I go to sleep. I wake up crying in the middle of the night because of it." Her voice was beginning to crack. "That's what my year has been like."

Nicholas makes a promise to his wife. He agrees that he will work with his son, as painfully slow as the process proves to be. Slowly, day by day, Ryan begins to make progress. He learns how to say "A" . . . then "ap" . . . then "apo." Sparks writes, "It was then that I began to cry. Simply to hear the sound of his voice, his voice—no screams, grunts, no shouts—was breathtaking. It was the sound of angels, as sweet as music. But more than that, I suddenly learned that Ryan could learn. And then I understood that this had been my greatest fear all along."

Then something amazing happened. While mom was away for vacation, Nicholas put Ryan on the phone. "I put the receiver up to Ryan's head, held out a little piece of candy, and mouthed the words I wanted him to say. The words we'd worked on all day long. And into the receiver, he said: 'I wuff you.' I love you. These were the first words Cat ever heard him say."[6]

We fumble and stammer when we come out of the waters of baptism. And begin to question whether or not our baptism really "took." We might wonder if we'll ever grow up spiritually, if we'll ever be able to tell God "I love you" with our lives.

The apostle knew the struggle involved in being an apprentice to Jesus. He understood the grit and the grime—the messiness of this path. He understood, as Ryan's parents do, that the process of becoming is painful and slow. But the Apostle Paul also knew that by God's spirit, the church, fumbling over the basics, could one day become so much more than she had been before. That even in our broken language, God recognizes the beauty of our efforts. And like the mother in love with her child, God desires for us to become who we were created to be. As we understand our individual and collective brokenness and the ways in which God heals us in baptism, we are in the process of becoming a church who understands herself as a priesthood of believers.

You might say to yourself, "I don't know Greek, or theology." You have been baptized. "I have my own doubts about God." You are being sustained in the the Lord's Supper. In these sacraments, God works with us, helping us learn the words we long to say.

One theologian says:

That is why, from very early on, Christian baptism was seen as the mode of entry into the Christian family, and why it was associated with the idea of being 'born again.' . . . The point is that the story which baptism tells is God's own story, from creation and covenant to new covenant and new creation, with Jesus in the middle of it and the Spirit brooding over it. In baptism, you are brought into that story, to be an actor in the play that God is writing and producing. And once you're onstage, you're part of the action. You can get the lines wrong. You can do your best to spoil the play. But the story is moving forward, and it would be far better to understand where it's going and how to learn your lines and join in the drama. *Through the water to become part of God's purpose for the world.*[7]

—⁓—

I'm certain that the Holy Communion was taught in a more robust way than I remember. As a child, I wasn't paying attention most of the time. Somewhere along the way, I got fixated on the supper of Christ as one thing: an act that focuses on the forgiveness of my sins. This was confusing for a young, naïve theologian such as me because only the baptized were allowed to take the meal of Jesus. Whatever your Saturday night vice happened to be, and I had *plenty*, the vices were no match for the power of the Lord's Supper—the deadly one-two punch in a thimble of grape juice, a few flakes of unleavened bread. (Or as one friend once said in a college class studying the historical meaning of the Eucharist, "I've just been tryin' to figure out why we don't take the Lord's Supper; we take the Lord's snack.") But eventually, I came to understand that faith shaped by these particular experiences with grape juice and crackers believes that God has brand new chapters for your life that are yet to be written. Though I can look back with amusement at government agents and white suits, it is this same church that has given me a robust understanding of the holy meal.

Both the meal and water remind Christians that Jesus is not a Socrates or Plato, dispensing moral nuggets of wisdom to better an already good life. Rather, the supper and baptism, I've been taught, remind us that Jesus is the suffering servant who invites us to the same kind of life. In taking the bread and the wine, and in the baptism of new believers, we confess our allegiance to the Kingdom of God over and above all others vying for our allegiance. In these sacraments, the church remembers that we've not only been forgiven but we've been restored by God's breath of life. Every Sunday, we are rehearsing the kinds of people we'll be throughout the rest of the week.

Every time the church gathers together, we remember that we are called to enact God's future into the present-day *mundane-ness* of right now. And we are, moment by moment, day by day, liberated from the false divisions that dominate our world.

There's food and there's *food*. There's water and there's *water*.

Grocery stores offer food and water. But I can take up the risky mission of Jesus because I've been baptized into a different story and I've received the food that gives me energy to be God's person in the world.

CHAPTER ELEVEN

KEEPING UP WITH THE JONESES

"Mo' money, mo' problems."
—UNKNOWN

*". . . Jesus' ministry with the poor, the prisoners, the blind and
broken victims is first and foremost a ministry of words. Jesus has
been anointed to preach, to proclaim the good news of release,
recovery, sight, liberty. He will, incidentally, do those things
before he is through, but from the beginning his ministry is not a
ministry of doing but a ministry of saying—what God has done,
what God is doing, what God will do. Everything that happens
in Jesus' ministry happens after proclamation and because of it,
because the speaking of God's word is how the world began and
how it goes on beginning, nourished and healed and strengthened
by the strong medicine of the gospel. . . . That is how it has been
working for almost two thousand years. That is how a Galilean
who spent his entire life in a country no bigger than New Jersey
became known around the world—all because people talk."*
—BARBARA BROWN TAYLOR

Paul dropped by my office not too long ago. I get drop-ins all the
time. It's one of my great daily challenges—to remember to be glad
to see someone when I have a list of ten things to do and five people to
call. I'm slow in learning that *actual* ministry usually happens when I
am on my way or preparing to do *official* ministry. Sometimes people
poke their heads in my office looking for directions to get around the

building. Sometimes the visitor is a dad looking for God's Helping Hands, our church's local food and clothing ministry. Other times, it's a young person who's run out of luck and needs some money to make it wherever he or she is going next. Occasionally, a person drops by announcing a pyramid scheme disguised as a "great business opportunity."

"Knock, knock," he said, as if I didn't hear his fist make contact with the door.

"I don't believe we've met," I quickly said.

"I'm Paul. You must be Josh," he replied. "Says so on the door!"

"Paul . . . hmmm . . . where are you from? Do you live here in town?"

"No, I don't live in these parts. I'm from a town you've never heard of."

"Try me."

"Okay. I'm from Tarsus. It used to be a place of some influence," he noted with a fair degree of pride. "Didn't spend too much time there, though."

"You're right. Never heard of it. Well, except for in the New . . . Testament . . . nah . . . never mind, that's crazy." I laughed a silent laugh.

An awkward pause filled the moment. Paul wasn't much to look at. He was short. His back hunched over a bit. He had an odd scar below his right eye, the kind you don't notice until the light catches his face just right. He squinted a lot, as if he'd left his glasses somewhere and was now trying to fake it. I noticed Paul looking at my desk. I had a few Bibles spread out with articles, commentaries, and personal notes.

Paul's eyes grew larger.

"Whatcha' working on?" he asked with genuine interest.

"Oh, I'm working on a chapter for a book I'm writing."

"Really?"

"Yep. I'm studying a pericope from Paul's letter to Timothy concerning money and wealth. We discussed poverty, suffering, forgiveness, justice, hope, and homelessness, but I know that any real discussion of spirituality has to deal with our addiction to attaining more."

"*Pericope*? That's a big word that means *passage*, right? How's it coming?"

"Do you know something about this letter?" Immediately, I wondered why I asked. If I've learned anything, it's that *shared* ignorance is still ignorance. And yet, strangely, I had a feeling this guy actually knew what he was talking about. Then he broke the brief silence.

"I know a bit, though others who've never met me or Timothy seem to know *more*. Never quite understood that, to be honest. That's true of all kinds of subjects."

"Do you mind if I ask you a few questions?" I blurted. This was an opportunity I could not pass up.

"All right. Let me guess. You want to talk about what I meant in my teaching about women and their role in the local church? Please tell me you're not stuck on my words about women being saved through childbearing?"

"No."

"You're curious to hear more thoughts on the role of elders and deacons?"

"That's not it either. Not today, anyway."

"Want to know more about the false teachers I combat in the letter? I really let them have it!"

He looked giddy.

"Actually, I was hoping you could elaborate a little more about your conviction that the love of money is 'a root of all kinds of evil.'"

"Ah, yes; you are a Generation X thinker, after all."

"Good point," I stammer, though I didn't know how this guy from the ancient Mediterranean world seemed so familiar with American culture.

"What are your questions?" he asked nonchalantly.

I dug in, preparing for a good conversation. Paul was in my office. My colleagues in the religion department where I teach would never believe this.

"I'm not sure if I believe that *money is the root of all kinds of evil*. That's a bold statement. What about pride, sex, hate, selfishness, jealousy, nationalism?"

I thought perhaps I stumped him. Maybe next time he'll poke his head in someone else's office. But Paul responded with great authority.

"I meant it. *Every* word. Here's the thing." As he spoke he leaned in, his intensity growing with each passing second. "So much is connected to money—power, sex, prestige, education, influence—it's all *connected* to money. I remember a group of hucksters in Ephesus who were using religion for financial gain. When I preached Christ crucified, the whole town broke into a riot."

"I remember that story! Luke told it in Acts. Let's see . . . what chapter was that?"

"Settle down. This isn't Bible Trivia Hour. I think what happened in Ephesus is a danger for Christians especially—to assume the acquisition of wealth as a sign of God's favor. I was in Borders the other day, waiting for a friend, and I noticed a book with the title *The Prayer of Jabez*. Have you read it?"

"Yes."

"It's dangerous nonsense. No disrespect to the author, I'm sure he's a great guy. I've never been one to mince words, you know. . . . Remember: I was beaten, shipwrecked, mocked, scourged, and penniless, without food, incarcerated. God never increased my territory. The closer I got to Jesus, the worse things got. It would not be a stretch to say that Jesus wrecked my life. I learned to be content in all things, but nothing about the gospel made my life easier."

"What's your rant got to do with 1 Timothy 6?"

"I'm speaking out of my own experience here. The lust for money leads you down all kinds of paths you never intended to travel. Wealth leads people into circles where the rules are different, the pressure is tremendous, and the values are totally blurred. What might have been unthinkable on the outside becomes quite natural on the inside. And the end of this way is utter devastation."

Flashbacks of family and friends who'd ruined their lives pursuing the almighty dollar filled my mind as he continued.

"I think it's called *keeping up with the Joneses*. Money is like salt water. 'Water, water everywhere, and not a drop to drink.' You think that it will quench your thirst, but actually it leaves you thirstier, not to mention empty. And the more you have, the more you have to lose. Remember the story of Joseph in Genesis? Why does Pharaoh have nightmares? Because those who have the most have the most anxiety about not having enough. So be wary of the people who are most anxious in your congregations. They have a lot to lose."[1]

I let his last line soak deep into my soul.

He continued, "Remember, though—I didn't say that wealth or the wealthy are inherently evil—I said that the love or all-consuming desire for money is the root of all kinds of evil."

That was a clarification I needed to understand, for in my youthful naiveté, I often forget this important truth.

"I want to say something about money and giving in this book I'm working on. In light of your experiences and writings, what wisdom do you want to share?" I wasn't going to let Paul out of my office without having him write a portion of this chapter. I'm young, but I'm no fool.

"Why do you think Christians don't give sacrificially?" he asked.

"My wife used to work at a restaurant when we were first married. The day she least liked to work was Sunday. Because Sunday afternoons were when the ornery, cheap Christians came into her restaurant. She got so tired of it; she started to work in the bar on Sundays."

Paul looked right through me. "I get your point. But let me give you some reasons why Christians are peculiar when it comes to their finances. First, some are in a bad spot. They've lost their jobs, which seems to be an increasing reality in your time. They are in serious financial debt, with credit cards extended beyond belief. Or they have maxed out their lifestyle to the point where the last place they are committed to is the local church."

"Can you explain that last part?"

"Sure. Let's say that you and your wife make forty thousand dollars a year. For a few years, you live off that money. Then, your wife gets a job and you are now making seventy thousand dollars total. The problem is in the lack of intentionality. Instead of living off fifty-five thousand and giving fifteen thousand, you now increase your lifestyle to live according to or beyond seventy thousand. Literally, the last thing you think about is how God's blessing can be used to expand the borders of his kingdom."

"What else?" I was now taking copious notes.

"Some don't give because they don't know any better. They haven't been challenged or taught; they haven't witnessed others giving. It's a foreign concept. You have to teach these things with grace and boldness.

"Others aren't generous, because, well . . . how do I say this? They're so busy building their own personal barns and empires that they have cold hearts toward the work of the local church. Money's like quicksand. You never see the trap coming—otherwise you'd avoid it. Once you get in the trap, it's almost impossible to get out. The harder you fight, the more likely you are to drown and suffocate. For instance, did you know that it is a documented fact that poor people in the United States give more than the wealthy? That's right, people who make less than twenty thousand dollars a year give a greater percentage of their wealth, on average, then those who make one hundred thousand dollars a year."[2]

"I'm not sure where to go from here."

"Here's how it's done," Paul said. "Tell local stories of people who've demonstrated great generosity. Don't tell stories about other people and other churches—tell the stories of God at work right where you are. You know the hardest place to live is right *where you are*? I've never understood preachers who don't, won't, or can't tell stories about what God is up to in their lives. How do they expect their churches to be able to do live faith out if they can't do it themselves?"

After processing the words of my wise friend and mustering some courage, I simply said, "I think I know what you mean. We have a family here in our church who demonstrated what this text would look like if it were taken seriously."

And now Paul was looking interested in what *I* had to say. Weird.

"Hurricane Katrina decimated the Gulf Coast of the United States—especially New Orleans. One family came from the devastated area to live in Detroit. My home church got wind of it. People came out of the woodwork to help the Johnson family. One family, in particular, made an indelible impression upon me. The husband walks up to me after one of our services and says, 'I have a car I want to give them. It's worth a good chunk of money, but I'd rather see it go to them.' Well, it turns out we could not get the car transferred to the family (the state of Michigan can be rather difficult), but this man was not deterred. He gave the displaced family enough money to pick out a quality and reliable minivan the next week.

"I also think of another story about people resisting the power of money. One family from my church went through several difficult circumstances. They waited in government line after government line. Ashamed. Frustrated. Scared. Their son was deathly ill; they were going through hard financial times. The church stepped up and helped them through their time of difficulty. They were so moved by this gesture that they started a ministry to help others in need, even though they lost their son to his sickness. Their idea, God's Helping Hands, started as a tiny closet and now resides in a large warehouse, where it's the largest single distributor of free food and clothing in one of Detroit's largest counties, providing hope for hundreds of the working poor in the Metro Detroit area."[3]

My new friend, the sage, paused and sat up slightly in his chair, taking a deep breath. He rested both hands upon his knees looking slightly down to the side.

"*Those* are the stories you tell. Those inspire others to think more intentionally about their orientation toward material possessions, greed, and giving . . . or lack thereof."

He'd done his work, and we both knew it.

"Thanks for dropping by," I said as I extended my hand in gratitude.

"No problem. Josh: You're a young leader like Timothy. I have to look out for you, make sure you don't say anything too stupid. You young preachers are like pitchers who throw a hundred miles an hour but don't always throw strikes. You might brush a few players back, and dazzle the one holding the radar gun . . . but that's not always the best thing. *Even still . . . let no one look down on you because you are young.*"

Then Paul looked at me with great seriousness.

"Tell *this* to anyone who might read your book. Make sure they know this message is from me.

Command those who are rich in this present world not to be arrogant nor to put their hope in wealth, which is so uncertain, but to put their hope in God, who richly provides us with everything for our enjoyment. Command them to do good, to be rich in good deeds, and to be generous and willing to share. In this way they will lay up treasure for themselves as a firm foundation for the coming age, so that they may take hold of the life that is truly life." (1 Timothy 6:17–19, NIV)

And with that, my theological confidant walked out of my office. I thought I owed it to you, the reader, to share the story of God's word breaking into my comfortable world. A Jesus Feast delivered right to my office.

CHAPTER TWELVE

AN INVITATION TO DANCE

"God is dead. God remains dead. And we have killed him. How shall we comfort ourselves, the murderers of all murderers? What was holiest and mightiest of all that the world has yet owned has bled to death under our knives: who will wipe this blood off us? What water is there for us to clean ourselves? What festivals of atonement, what sacred games shall we have to invent? Is not the greatness of this deed too great for us? Must we ourselves not become gods simply to appear worthy of it?"
—NIETZSCHE, *The Gay Science*

"In the end, there's a divinity that shapes our ends, rough-hew them how we may."
—SHAKESPEARE (Abraham Lincoln's favorite quote about God)

The innovative Christian leader, Bill Hybels, recently wrote these interesting words regarding the areas of Christian discipleship Willow Creek Church (an influential church in Chicago) should have paid more attention to as they grew from a small church into one of the largest churches in the United States. "We should have gotten people, taught people, how to read their Bible between services, how to do the spiritual practices more aggressively on their own. In other words, spiritual growth doesn't happen best by becoming dependent on elaborate church programs but through the age old spiritual practices of prayer, Bible-reading, and relationships."[1] Leaders have failed, Hybels said, to teach followers of Jesus the spiritual disciplines of the church.

One truth we can be certain of: following Jesus isn't easy. The brain surgeon, Olympic athlete, and accomplished violinist have one significant thing in common: years of discipline and study in mastering their particular crafts.

As apprentices of Jesus, our *craft* is to mimic the life and teachings of Jesus. That is what one strives to embody in this complicated and confusing world. A Christian's first calling— regardless of whether we choose to spend our time as a mother, lawyer, teacher, pastor, or nuclear physicist—is to live in a *mystical relationship* with the living Jesus. But this takes work. One respected thinker in Christianity was asked by a minister about his daily routine. This leader responded, "I've learned that discipline is my best friend. I have always been suspicious of the easy way."[2] Throughout this book, we've talked about risk-taking, forgiveness, suffering, radical hospitality, caring for the broken and poor—the only way these feats are accomplished in our world and for our world is by rooting oneself in a daily rhythm, a cadence that mirrors Jesus himself.

Consider Paul's wisdom regarding discipleship. Philippians 2:12 and following is a pastoral encouragement to a group of Christians living under the Roman shadow of Caesar—those followers of the Way living in Philippi. These words are a meal to be digested:

Therefore, my dear friends, as you have always obeyed—not only in my presence, but now much more in my absence—continue to work out your salvation with fear and trembling, for it is God who works in you to will and to act in order to fulfill his good purpose. (NIV)

Paul seems to think, contrary to some teachings in today's religious culture, that salvation is a collective process. This encouragement could read, "*Y'all* continue to work out *all y'all's* salvation."[3]

Paul also seems to think, in the larger context of this letter, that salvation is *more* than avoiding hell or being "right with God"—for

Paul, salvation is the abiding relationship one has with Christ. "Being like Christ," "putting on Christ," and "in Christ" are all phrases demonstrating the truth that God's desire for humanity is to experience life in very specific ways. Thus, to be "saved" is to be rescued from one way of being human into another way. Christians are empowered by the Spirit to become like Jesus. We are invited to come closer to God in our bond with Jesus.

—///—

Spiritual disciplines are the daily means by which we come into contact with God. These practices do not ensure a magical appearance of God, as if God is a genie in a bottle waiting for us to rub the bottle the right way. Rather, these disciplines give us the eyes to see the way in which God is closer to us than we are to ourselves. The key element in understanding disciplines is this: they are not rules or practices one must follow in order to be "saved." Spiritual disciplines create space for the Holy Spirit to work anew, changing us in steady ways. My friend, Rabbi Mark Kinzer, once reminded me, "Josh, keeping Torah is not a burden. Keeping Torah is a blessing. It is true freedom, for it is life-giving."

Lauren Winner further explains what Rabbi Kinzer believes in her book on spiritual formation, *Mudhouse Sabbath*:

Jews do these things with more attention and wisdom not because they are more righteous nor because God likes them better, but rather because doing, because action, sits at the center of Judaism. Practice is to Judaism what belief is to Christianity. That is not to say that Judaism doesn't have dogma or doctrine. It is rather to say that, for Jews, the essence of the thing is a doing, an action. Your faith might come and go, but your practice ought not waver . . . This is perhaps best explained by a *midrash* (a rabbinic commentary on a biblical text). This *midrash* explains a curious turn of phrase in the Book of Exodus: "Na'aseh v'nishma," which means "we

will do and we will hear" or "we will do and we will understand," a phrase drawn from Exodus 24, in which the people of
Israel proclaim, "All the words that God has spoken, we will do
and we will hear." The word order, the rabbis have observed,
doesn't seem to make any sense: How can a person obey God's
commandment before they hear it? But the counterintuitive
lesson, the *midrash* continues, is precisely that one acts out
God's commands, one does things unto God, and eventually,
through the doing, one will come to hear and understand and
believe. In this *midrash*, the rabbis have offered an apology for
spiritual practice, for doing.[4]

Spiritual disciplines are the things we do to connect us to God. Several
different disciplines sustain me. These disciplines create space for the
holy to replace the chaos. I hope you hear the etymological connection
of *discipline* and *disciple*.

Many have compared a relationship with God to dancing. And I realize that dancing and church mix about as well as a yellow-dog Democrat
and a libertarian or a George W. Bush appearance at an initiation party
for European pacifists. The dance metaphor might get me tarred and
feathered by some, but I think I have the Psalms on my side on this one
with phrases like, "You have turned my mourning into dancing."

My wife and I have taken dance lessons, which were at times frus-
trating and awkward. I can testify that dancing reveals much about
one's spiritual disposition—one's posture before humanity and the
Divine. Dancing opens our imaginations up to see the world as God
sees it.

Obviously, for the sake of this discussion, God is leading us in this
spiritual dance. But he cannot dance unless we are willing to trust and
move with him. Therefore, as the expression goes, in our spiritual lives
it certainly does take two to tango. God does not seem interested in
forcing himself on people. Rather, God honors both our willingness to
engage as well as our propensity to rebel and pull away.

It is one thing to know *about* God (fact, doctrines, proofs, or formulas). It is quite another thing to *know God*. It is one thing to explain God as if he were contained in a laboratory. It is another thing altogether to have been in God's unmistakable presence. Dancing with God is perhaps the most rewarding dance of all, for we become the person God already knows us to be.[5] I invite you to consider some of the dance steps I've learned through spending time with Jesus and his church: Sabbath. Exercise. Reading. Giving. Solidarity with the poor. Confession.

Sabbath

We dance in rhythm with God when we keep the Sabbath. The reason we are called to take a day of rest is simple. Humans tend to forget that we did not make the world and, thus, that the world does not depend upon us. Barbara Brown Taylor tells a story about a friend, David, growing up in Atlanta and what he taught her about fidelity to God.

> When I was a junior in high school, my boyfriend Herb played on the varsity basketball team. He was not the star player however. The star player was a boy named David, who scored so many points during his four-year career that the coach retired his jersey when he graduated. This would have been remarkable under any circumstances, but it was doubly so since David did not play on Friday nights. On Friday nights, David observed the Sabbath with the rest of his family, who generously withdrew when David's gentile friends arrived, sweaty and defeated, after Friday night home games.

Following each Friday night game, David's friends came to his house to describe the game in great detail. "Blow by blow" the gentiles were allowed to speak and create worlds in David's living room. Someone in the room asked if it bothered him to sit at home while his team "was getting slaughtered in the high school gymnasium."

"No one makes me do this," he said. "I'm a Jew, and Jews observe the Sabbath." Six days a week, he said, he loved nothing more than playing basketball and he gladly gave all he had to the game. On the seventh day, he loved being a Jew more than he loved playing basketball, and he just as gladly gave all he had to the Sabbath. Sure, he felt a tug, but that was the whole point. Sabbath was his chance to remember what was really real. Once three stars were visible in the Friday night sky, his identity as a Jew was more real to him than his identity as the star of our basketball team.[6]

It is essential for Christians to create regular, intentional spaces of time in which we do not work, email, fax, clean, or do laundry. A time when we allow our hearts to settle and the voices to hush. Sabbath is a time when we remember that God made the world and rested; that he calls us to rest with him, to hear his voice, to be aware of his presence. And it is a time to remember, according to the Hebrew Testament teaching on Sabbath and Jubilee, that there will be a day when all peoples of the world will rest—not just the ones who can financially afford to take a day off.[7]

Sabbath-keeping reminds us that we are pilgrims in a foreign land, awaiting the world to become what the world was meant to be. We remember vividly that, although God made the world, the world is not the way God made it. When we keep Sabbath, we proclaim to the rest of the world that God is about the business of making things new. God needs a way of reminding us that we are no longer in Egypt, stacking bricks for the Empire. If busyness and idolatry plague our collective life, Sabbath is a means by which we can become more like the person God created us to be.

For the last few years, I've rigorously worked to keep a full Sabbath day in my weekly schedule. It hasn't always been easy. Deaths, births, tragedies, miracles, and mundane duties of life show little regard for my personal desire to rest. Slowly, over time, when those things occur on Sabbath, I'm tempted to jump in and fix everything. Sometimes, when the circumstances demand, I have to get involved. Most of the time, however, keeping Sabbath convicts me that the world can run just fine without me. I see a clear role for myself in the divine story. I am important in this narrative, but I'm not the main point or the main character. Sabbath teaches me this.

Whole.

Rested.

Listening.

Attentive.

Cleansed.

This is what Sabbath is about. It creates the space in our lives for us to remember who we are. To remember that we are players in a different story.

Exercise

I often think about how much life has changed from the 1940s, when my grandfather was a fifteen-year-old running the family farm in rural Cullman, Alabama, as compared to my life growing up as a fifteen-year-old in the mid-90s in the cozy confines of a large suburban metropolis. My rhythm of life could not have been more different than previous generations. In a world of iPods, email, Facebook, Internet grocery shopping, five hundred plus cable channels, On Demand, HDTV, DVR, and DVDs, there's not a great deal of opportunity for the physical body to be challenged and exerted.

I've competed in a triathlon and marathon over the last few years. Most people believe that the race day is the highlight. Not true. The race day is usually a letdown. What I cherish most are the moments when my discipline overcame my desire to take the easy path.

I remember a Friday morning when I ran twenty miles in the pouring rain with my friend and trainer, Andy. I remember the leg cramps I endured the days following long races. I remember getting up early on days when I wanted to do nothing more than sleep in.

Care of the body is essential to a holistic life. As Rob Bell reminds us in *Sex God*: "We are not animals, bodies with no soul. We are not angels, spirits lacking a body. We are both body and spirit." Exercise keeps our whole person in rhythm; it keeps us in step with the Holy One.

Reading

I am trying to be a "middle reader."[8] By that I mean a person who reads about all kinds of subjects from various perspectives. This is my biggest beef with some Christian pastors and ministers—they come out of graduate school sounding removed. Yet, Jesus spoke in parables, with earthy analogies and parallels. As I write this you will find on my nightstand a novel by John Steinbeck, a book on preaching from the early 1900s by Karl Barth, a book about marriage, and a biography of George Washington. Reading ushers us into foreign worlds. Becoming a middle reader ensures that we do not convince ourselves that we are the central characters in God's plot. Hemmingway's *The Sun Also Rises* takes me to Madrid in the early twentieth century. I'm there. I can smell the city streets and the bulls. Steinbeck's *East of Eden* teaches me what it means to be a human connected to the land. Being a middle reader keeps me connected to *all* humanity, not just the humans I tend to gravitate toward in daily life.

Reading widely also teaches us to read the Bible anew. Rather than reading it as a rule-book or document full of timeless principles, like mining a river for gold nuggets, we fall in love with the Bible because we realize the Author is the main character, and that we've been invited to *live* in this story. Rather than mastering Scripture, we slowly become mastered by it. God commands Ezekiel to eat his words, and the prophet does so. Jeremiah delights in eating the words of God. In Revelation, John is instructed to "eat this book." Consume it, let it change the way you see the world. Let it become a part of your very bones and muscles. "The Bible is a most comforting book; it is also a most discomforting book," Eugene Peterson observes. "Eat this book; it will be sweet as honey in your mouth; but it will also be bitter to your stomach. You can't reduce this book to what you can handle; you can't domesticate this book to what you are comfortable with. You can't make it your toy poodle, trained to respond to your commands."[9]

Giving

My wife and I made a decision that we would give ten percent to our church, and give to other causes over and above our commitment to the local church. We can quibble over the Old Testament/New Testament teachings on tithing, but that's not the dog I'm chasing. When the average Christian in the United States gives less than three percent, arguing over "before tax" and "after tax" distinctions seems a bit foolish and futile, like rearranging furniture on the Titanic.

In a culture of affluence, one of the most countercultural acts one can embark upon is to consistently give money to efforts that do not bring you financial benefit. The last commandment in the Decalogue is still one that Christians need to remember: "You shall not covet your neighbor's house. You shall not covet your neighbor's wife, or his man-servant or maidservant, his ox or donkey, or anything that belongs to your neighbor." Giving what already belongs to God is a simple way of ensuring that we not covet or find our identity in what we have and don't have. Instead, we focus on what God has already provided.

Solidarity with the Poor

I try to spend time with the "least of these" every week. Granted, poverty comes in emotion, spirit, and body. Yet, for this season of my life, I feel called to those people who are economically oppressed. Here are my primary reasons. First, it's a command and expectation in Torah, the Prophets, and Jesus.[10] Drinking and gambling are not as important to Jesus as life with the poor. Second, I want the prejudices and stereotypes that I possess to be exposed and dealt with on a weekly basis. Third, and most important: in my work with the poor, I have come to have a clearer picture of Jesus—the jobless, penniless, homeless itinerant preacher who came from Nazareth talking about the "kingdom of God."

Confession

Each week I meet with five other men and we confess our sins to each other. It isn't that I believe my friends possess the ability to forgive me of my sins, but I don't know how to live a forgiven life outside of a community that hears what I need forgiveness for in the first place. Dietrich Bonhoeffer suggests that "confession is the beginning of discipleship." In confessing the darkness that rages within, I start to become whole and transparent.

During his college days, noted contemporary author Donald Miller concocted the crazy idea to put up a confession booth on the secular (and somewhat anti-Christian) campus of Reed College in Oregon. His timing was a bit awkward. He wanted to set up shop during *Ren Fayre*, a time of drinking, drug use, and orgies. Instead of asking other students to confess their sins (something Christians are curiously good at), Miller led the experiment by offering a confession of his own sins, as well as the past sins of Christianity. He writes: "You never question the truth of something until you have to explain it to a skeptic. I didn't feel like being in the booth or wearing that stupid monk outfit. I wanted to go to the rave. Everybody in there was cool, and we were just religious. I was just going to tell Tony that I didn't want to do it when he opened the curtain and said we had our first customer." The conversation went like this:

> "What's up, man?" Duder sat himself on the chair with a smile on his face. He told me my pipe smelled good.
>
> "Thanks," I said. I asked him his name, and he said his name was Jake. I shook his hand because I didn't know what to do, really.
>
> "So, what is this? I'm supposed to tell you all of the juicy gossip I did at Ren Fayre, right?" Jake said.

"No."

"Okay, then what? What's the game?" He asked.

"Not really a game. More of a confession thing."

"You want me to confess my sins, right?"

"No, that's not what we're doing, really."

"What's the deal, man? What's with the monk outfit?"

"Well, we are, well, a group of Christians here on campus, you know."

"I see. Strange place for Christians, but I am listening."

"Thanks," I told him. He was being very patient and gracious. "Anyway, there is a group of us, just a few of us who were thinking about the way Christians have wronged people over time."

After haggling over the intent, Jake finally began to understand. The conversation took a serious turn once Jake realized that this was a life-giving proposition.

"So, you are confessing to me!" Jake said with a laugh.

"Yeah. We are confessing to you. I mean, I am confessing to you."

"You're serious." His laugh turned to something of a straight face.

I told him I was. He looked at me and told me I didn't have to. I told him I did, and I felt very strongly in that moment that I was supposed to tell Jake that I was sorry about everything."

After confessing for a good while, Jake became empowered. His compassion increased with each passing second. Here we understand the power within the act of confession.

"It's all right, man," Jake said, very tenderly. His eyes starting to water.

"Well," I said, clearing my throat, "I am sorry for all of that."

"I forgive you," Jake said. And he meant it.[11]

The two talked for a little longer about the essence of the Christian story, and Donald shared with Jake the simple, but not easy, story of grace as found in the gospel. And, wouldn't you know, Jake told many of his friends that they needed to visit the Christians in the confession booth. I can just imagine that conversation. "You won't believe what those Christians are up to now!"

—⁓—

As one who cares for the souls of many Christians and non-Christians alike, several things break my heart. My heart is broken when I spend time with children who grow up bouncing from shelter to shelter in Detroit. My heart breaks when I see what alcohol addiction has done to the lives of promising and talented young men. My heart shatters when I see what bulimia and anorexia can to do the body and soul of a woman. I'm crushed when I witness the power of sexual addiction and the destruction it causes in some of the marriages I see.

But perhaps the thing that breaks my heart the most is one you would not expect. I'm heartbroken for those who spend much of their lives as "practical atheists." A *practical atheist* may or not believe in the existence of God—that is inconsequential. A practical atheist is one who fails to see the work of God in the different episodes of life. A practical atheist believes that God has left us alone and is no longer interested in the affairs of our lives. A practical atheist does not believe in the power of God to transform lives. Practical atheists tend to hide in church, knowing many things about God without realizing God's power.

I recall listening to a dialog between a Christian minister and a thoughtful atheist. Actually the second person was more an agnostic than atheist (*not* knowing whether or not God exists is, in fact, different than *knowing* that God does not exist). This odd couple discussed the various churches they visited over the course of several months. They went to some of the largest and most influential churches in

America. Churches that you would know if I listed them. They also visited smaller, out-of-the-way congregations.

The agnostic said one thing that I can't forget.

When asked about which churches influenced him the most spiritually (right now you might be thinking, "What authority does an agnostic have concerning spiritual matters?"), the agnostic responded with humility, "I was most touched by the churches that challenged me. There were plenty of churches that had great worship, teaching, drama, arts, and music. But I appreciated the churches that asked me to do something in God's world."[12]

In Jesus of Nazareth, God has invited each and every person to a holy dance. Some have been dancing by themselves and wonder from whence comes the loneliness. Some have danced with too many partners to remember and are jaded. Others have stayed on the sideline, hovering over the punch bowl.

In practicing the spiritual disciplines I've now described, one can slowly become more in tune with the living God.

God is not dead. When others rub shoulders with you, they will know that to be true. They will come to know that *practical atheism* is bankrupt. They will know intimately and up close that God is alive and well, working in the lives of those who have learned to dance on holy ground.

All because you've feasted on the words of Jesus, who reminds us that his way is good, just, and whole, for his yoke is easy and his burden is light.

THE FEAST

Humans know suffering and disillusionment. Everyone knows pain. Young boys and girls in Northern Uganda are used as child soldiers to fight the wars of their parents. Large numbers of teens in suburban America are addicted to meth. Loved ones come down with strange medical conditions never to return to their normal status. Spouses of several decades suddenly disappear. Men betray women, and women disdain men. People in the same family hate one another. The resurrection of Jesus swallows these realities and gives us a new vision of how life can be.

God did not delete evil and suffering from the world; God transformed the evil of this world by letting his Son be nailed to a tree. God did not rid the world of death; instead, God joins us in our suffering and overcomes its sting by raising his Son from the dead.

The Christian receives *hope* from an empty tomb and *identity* from the one who walked away from death with scars as permanent reminders of his unfailing love. "For no greater love is there than the one who would lay down his life for another." And no greater joy now remains for the one who rises from the dead than to breathe new life into our weary souls. One day, we will be with those who've had their lives cut short. Through faith, God changes the world and brings dead people back to life.

It might surprise you to think about Martin Luther King, Jr., as an artist, but that's precisely what he was. He used words to change the hearts and imaginations of people all over the world. That's what artists do—they use their gift to inspire and prompt, challenging the way we conceive reality. Artists challenge us to creatively and courageously engage the world around us.

In the aftermath of one of this nation's great tragedies (the bombing of three young girls), Dr. King delivered these words at Sixth Avenue Baptist Church on September 18, 1963, in Birmingham, Alabama. These words sustain me in my moments of deep awareness of the pain that plagues our world. These words go everywhere I go. These words have become a part of my soul.

Death comes to every individual. There is an amazing democracy about death. It is not an aristocracy for some of the people, but a democracy for all of the people. Kings die and beggars die; rich men and poor men die; old people die and young people die. Death comes to the innocent and it comes to the guilty. Death is the irreducible common denominator of all men.

I hope you can find some consolation from Christianity's affirmation that death is not the end. Death is not a period that ends the great sentence of life, but a comma that punctuates it to more lofty significance. Death is not a blind alley that leads the human race into a state of nothingness, but an open door which leads man into life eternal. Let this daring faith, this great invincible surmise, be your sustaining power during these trying days.

. . . Life is hard, at times as hard as crucible steel. It has its bleak and difficult moments. Like the ever-flowing waters of the river, life has its moments of drought and its moments of flood. Like the ever-changing cycle of the seasons, life has the soothing warmth of its summers and the piercing chill of its winters. And if one will hold on, he will discover that God walks with him, and that God is able to lift you from the fatigue of despair to the buoyancy of hope, and transform dark and desolate valleys into sunlit paths of inner peace.[1]

There is a day coming when God will raise all women and men from the dead.

Ultimately, all of us are artists in the sense that we can create worlds of chaos or worlds of peace. We have the potential to create love or hate, truth or deceit, forgiveness or revenge.

If it's true that we are artists, our lives are our portfolios. *God's gift is one's life. What one does with one's life is one's gift back to God.* When we offer our lives back to him, we can pause from our wrestling, if only for a moment, and enjoy the sweet embrace of God.

A day of resurrection is on its way.

Professor Jack and Anne from Cass Park, Bonhoeffer, Dr. King, Mother Teresa, Benny, Nic Paradise, you . . . me . . . all of us will stand before the love and mercy of God. And for the very first time, we will be a part of the perfect feast.

It's a party like we've never seen.

Everyone's invited.

To believe this requires a powerful, God-initiated imagination. When our imaginations are stirred we believe in a different kind of world.

A world altered because God makes sense of the mess.

A world that rewards risk.

A world over-flowing with God's justice and mercy.

A world soaked in reconciliation.

A world full of people dancing with God.

Until this world is fully manifested, may those who follow the teachings of the Rabbi from Nazareth conduct and share Jesus Feasts all around the world, in every imaginable space. With our bellies full of Jesus and his teachings, we go into the world with energy to sustain our witness and conversations. In every space and in every moment, we bring the prayer of Jesus to fruition: that *his* way of being human would be experienced on earth as it *already* is being done in the realm of heaven.

Near the end of Jesus' life, when he first instituted *the* Jesus Feast, he tells his disciples that he "eagerly desired" to share in the meal that commemorates God's liberation of humanity from sin, death, darkness, and the powers that be. He continues by telling his disciples that he will not take of the Jesus Feast until the day when all things are made new, and heaven and earth become one (Luke 22:14–16).[2]

Because we've feasted on Jesus, we cling to the belief that should this world and this life kill us, the one thing we need is the one thing God has already promised: *I will raise you from the dead.*

God is more for us than we are for ourselves. For most of our lives we've worried about trying to work God into our stories. The entire time, God was inviting us to join *his*. Faith in the postmodern world is not mere belief in the existence of God. Authentic faith is the conviction that God makes new from old, life from death, hope from darkness, *a way out of no way.* Deep spirituality is being able to imagine the world, not as it *is*, but as it *will be.*

Imagine that.

ACKNOWLEDGMENTS

I am grateful to my wife, Kara, who understands my passion for reading and writing and who is the nearest gospel experience in my life. That she looks at me with half the love and adoration I have for her is something I'll never quite comprehend. Thank you.

I'm indebted to Greg Taylor, senior editor of *New Wineskins Magazine*, for the editing he's provided in much of my writing over the last several years—as well as careful attention to this work. Thank you for helping to clarify my voice and give me the confidence to continue to write with passion and precision. Also, Leonard Allen saw the possibilities of this book from the beginning. I'm eternally grateful.

Every member of the Graves family gave me confidence to pursue my own writing voice. I pray my life reciprocates this gesture.

Several people read early versions of *The Feast*: Sara Barton, Josh Ross, Dorothy Hause, Dana Spivy, along with an adult formation class at Rochester Church of Christ. Your attention to detail is remarkable.

For my friends who live, hope, and struggle in Cass Corridor— thank you for blessing me for the last few years. I will value your wisdom, transparency, and communion for the rest of my life. Jack and Anne (rest in peace), Francis, Diane, Vivian, Aleya, and Winzell—you are God's beloved children. This book would not have been written if not for your friendship, perspective, and insight.

I do not write for scholars, for this work is not meant to be erudite. I do not primarily write this book even for my fellow ministers and pastors, though I hope this will bless them in some small way.

I write this book for young adults who now live in a global society. I write for the missional-minded leader. I write for the doctor trying to be faithful in her practice of medicine in the urban hospital. I write this for the college student contemplating walking away from Christianity to other forms of spiritual expression. I write this for the single dad trying to make it one more day. I write this for the Christians living in Jinja, Uganda, living the life of Jesus in the midst of poverty. I write this for those men and women who, as in the time of the first century, are turning the world upside down because their bellies are full of *gospel* food.

ENDNOTES

Introduction: Spiritual Anorexia

1 See Dietrich Bonhoeffer, *Life Together: The Classic Exploration of Faith in Community* (New York: HarperOne, 2003), which is the twentieth-century standard for practical theology and the shared-life experience.

2 Quoted in Michael Frost and Alan Hirsch's *The Shaping of Thing to Come: Innovation and Mission for the 21st-Century Church* (Boston: Hendrickson, 2003), 101.

3 Eugene Peterson, *Eat this Book: A Conversation in the Art of Spiritual Reading* (Grand Rapids: Zondervan, 2007), 18. Of course, Peterson is not the first or only person to use this metaphor. Barbara Brown Taylor's books, *Feasting on the Word* (2008), *Seeds of Heaven* (2004), and *Bread of Angels* (1997) also employ this understanding of the biblical text.

4 See the documentary entitled *Theologians Under Hitler: Could it Happen Again?* by Steven D. Martin, Vital Visuals, 2005.

5 Thomas Hardy, "Christmas 1924," *Thomas Hardy: The Complete Poems* (New York: Palgrave, 2002), 914.

6 See Philip Jenkins outstanding trilogy on the emerging shape of global Christianity: *The New Faces of Christianity: Believing the Bible in the Global South* (New York: Oxford Press, 2006); *The Next Christendom: The Coming of Global Christianity* (New York: Oxford Press, 2007); and *God's Continent: Christianity, Islam, and Europe's Religious Crisis* (New York: Oxford Press, 2007). Also, Brian D. McLaren's *Everything Must Change: Jesus, Global Crises, and a Revolution of Hope* (Nashville: Thomas Nelson, 2007) is one of the more constructive blueprints for the church's local and global mission in our pluralistic society.

7 Stan Grenberg (Executive Director of Kairos Church Planting Network) writes: "Since about 1985 Churches of Christ in America have been on a growth plateau—same number of churches (about 13,000), same number of members (1,300,000). Consider this though. In 1985 the US population was 238 million people. Today it is near 306 million people. That is roughly a 30% increase. That means for the past twenty-three years while we stayed at our 1985 size our impact on the people around us decreased by 30%."

8 "An Interview with Brian McLaren," *New Wineskins* (2008). You can read or listen to the entire interview online at http://www.wineskins.org/filter. asp?SID=2&fi_key=149&co_key=1579.

Chapter One: Making Sense of the Mess

1 I also read recently that in some regions of ancient Mesopotamia, *buoyancy* was used in disputed cases of sexual indiscretion. If the accused couple floated while thrown into a river, they were innocent and thus lived to tell about it. If the accused drowned, they were guilty (how convenient!) and thus perished as a result of their deceit. When I asked Walter Brueggemann about this he responded, "Can one float in dung?" I had that coming, I suppose.

Chapter Two: Theotokos

1 Several writers have addressed this in recent years. I must give credit especially to Scot McKnight, since much of this section is directly linked to his work and thinking in *Jesus Creed: Loving God, Loving Others* (Brewster, MA: Paraclete Press, 2004).

2 Barbara Brown Taylor, *Gospel Medicine* (Boston: Cowley Press, 1995), 156–157.

3 Ibid., 153. In this chapter, Taylor unpacks, in ways that only she is able to do, the significance of Mary as the *theotokos*—the one who bears God into the world.

4 I recently watched the film, *The Nativity Story* (New Line Cinema, 2007). This *midrash* depiction of the Birth of Jesus gives special attention to Joseph and Mary and is an excellent artistic interpretation of the life Joseph and Mary endured to bring Jesus into the world. I was particularly struck by two elements of the film: the social isolation that Mary and Joseph must have endured, and the political threat that Jesus' birth represented over and against the throne of Herod (the extension of Rome's imperial power in Israel).

Chapter Three: Wrestling with the Real Jesus

1 Charles L. Campbell has written a provocative book, *The Word on the Street: Performing the Scriptures in the Urban Context* (Grand Rapids: Eerdmans, 2000). Campbell is one of the most important voices regarding the relationship of preaching and ethics in postmodern culture. He teaches at Duke Divinity School in North Carolina.

2 Taylor Branch, *Parting the Waters: America during the King Years, 1954–1963* (New York: Simon & Schuster, 1989).

3   Quoted in James Wm. McClendon, Jr.'s *Biography as Theology: How Life Stories Can Remake Today's Theology* (Nashville: Abingdon, 1974), 89–113.

4   Of course, by "in-breaking reign" I mean the kingdom (*basileia*). This word, *basileia*, can be understood as the rule, way, reign, or intent of God. For example, "The kingdom of God is near"—this phrase means that the *way* of God is now present in the person and work of Jesus. Jesus is teaching humanity what it means to be truly human. As Lee Camp has written, "it is not through the power brokers of human history that God will effect God's purposes, but through the little minority band of peoples committed to walking in the way of Jesus of Nazareth, bearing witness to the new reality, the new creation, the kingdom of God. And all this requires, besides, great trust: that it is not our task to make things turn out right but instead to be faithful witnesses. We will have to trust that God will be God, and do what God has promised" (*Mere Discipleship* [Grand Rapids: Brazos Press, 2003], 59).

5   See N. T. Wright, *Surprised by Hope: Rethinking Heaven, the Resurrection, and the Mission of the Church* (San Francisco: HarperOne, 2008).

6   Eugene Peterson, *Christ Plays in Ten Thousand Places: A Conversation in Spiritual Theology* (Grand Rapids: Eerdmans, 2005), 134–136.

7   Repent (in the Greek, *metanoia*): to turn, change, or alter the course of one's life in belief and behavior. Repentance is just as much a statement of *opportunity* in the Gospels as it is a statement of *judgment* (c.f. Mark 1:14–15).

8   John Howard Yoder, *The Original Revolution* (Scottdale, Pennsylvania: Herald Press, 1971), 13–33. See also N. T. Wright, *The New Testament and the People of God* (London: SPCK, 1996). Wright's work deals with the background information of Judaism's sects quite well. I use these options as a grid of sorts for engaging culture (film, music, etc.) with my students at Rochester College. First, one can create a moral society based upon a fragmented and reductionistic ethical code (the Pharisee option). Or, one can buy wholesale what Rome is serving up (the Sadducee option). Third, one can declare war on Rome, which, of course, is the zealot option. Fourth, one can seek to create a radical community completely separate from the rest of the world (the Essene option). Though all of those options show up in modern Christian epistemology and praxis, I choose the Jesus option: incarnation. In this option, I enter into the suffering and chaos of the world, while maintaining a holy disposition by the power of God's Spirit.

9   See Rob Bell's *Velvet Elvis: Repainting the Christian Faith* (Grand Rapids: Zondervan, 2005), 166, for an excellent popular commentary on the idea of the gospel being "good news" for contemporary culture.

10 I give credit to David Fleer for the phrase "reforming center of Christianity."

11 Philip Yancey, *What's So Amazing About Grace?* (Grand Rapids: Zondervan, 1997), 48–49.

12 Shane Claiborne's *The Irresistible Revolution: Living as an Ordinary Radical* (Grand Rapids: Zondervan, 2006) is a challenging and provocative book about the shape of discipleship in the American context.

13 For a great theological exposition of discipleship for the postmodern world, see C. Leonard Allen, *Things Unseen: Churches of Christ in (and after)*

the Modern Era (Siloam Springs, Arkansas: Leafwood Publishers, 2004), 157–180.

Chapter Four: The Greatest Risk

1   I have told this story before in other settings. One: because it's funny. Two: because it exposes my worldview. By the way, this story in no way is intended to undermine or downplay the importance of professional and pastoral counseling.

2   Taken from Scot McKnight's blog, *Jesus Creed*, which appears on beliefnet and which you can read at http://blog.beliefnet.com/jesuscreed/.

3   See Tony Hendra, *The Messiah of Morris Avenue* (New York: Henry Holt and Company, 2006), 167. This novel asks a simple question: If Jesus came to judge and re-imagine the religion of ancient Judaism, what would it look like if he were to do the same thing to modern American Christianity? This is not a Christian novel *per se* (as that term has come to be defined), but it is one of the more thoughtful modern expositions of the radical otherness of Jesus' life and teachings. Tony Hendra re-imagines a conversation with Jesus and the rich young man that dares to describe what Jesus might look like in 2007 America.

4   See Philippians 1:2. Which also reminds me of Paul's words in 2 Corinthians 11:23–30: ". . . I have worked much harder, been in prison more frequently, been flogged more severely, been exposed to death and death again. Five times I received from the Jews the forty lashes minus one. Three times I was beaten with rods, once I was stoned, three times I was shipwrecked, I spent a night and a day in the open sea, I have been constantly on the move. I have been in danger from rivers, in danger from bandits, in danger from own countrymen, in danger from the Gentiles, in danger in the city, in danger in the country, in danger at sea; and in danger from false brothers. I have labored and toiled and have often gone without sleep; I have known hunger and thirst and have often gone without food; I have been cold and naked . . . . If I must boast, I will boast of the things that show my weakness."

5   Daniel de Roulet's *Finding Your Plot in a Plotless World: A Little Direction* (Grand Rapids: Brazos, 2007) is a great resource for carrying forth this discussion with young adults wrestling with vocation, as well as more seasoned veterans who find themselves at a crossroad.

6   From Sara Barton's lecture, "How Jesus Wrecked My Life," which she delivered at Rochester College, Fall 2006.

Chapter Five: Can I Get a Witness?

1   You can read more about Jeremiah Cummings on his ministry home page at http://www.wicctv.org. Be sure to check out the link labeled "My Testimony."

2 Malcolm X, *The Autobiography of Malcolm X* (New York: Grove Press, 1964). For a fascinating analysis of the resurgence of Malcolm X in American culture, see Michael Eric Dyson's *Making Malcolm: The Myth and Meaning of Malcolm X* (New York: Oxford University Press, 2005). His chapter "Spike's Malcolm" (129–144) is worth the price of the book.

3 Richard Lischer, *The Preacher King: Martin Luther King Jr. and the Word that Moved America* (New York: Oxford Press, 1995), 181. Lischer's entire section on prophets and Martin Luther King's prophetic role in America is outstanding (see pp. 173–194).

4 See, for examples, Genesis 50:22ff; Exodus 3:19, 6:1ff, 15; Deuteronomy 7, 30:1ff; Nehemiah 9:9.

5 *Malcolm X*, 9–10. Malcolm also has this to say regarding his father's death: "As I began to be recognized more around the town, I started to become aware of the peculiar attitude of white people toward me. I sensed that it had to do with my father. It was an adult version of what several children had said at school, in hints, or sometimes in the open, which really expressed what their parents had said—that the Black Legion of Klan had killed my father, and the insurance company had pulled a fast one in refusing to pay my mother the policy money" (p. 15).

6 Ibid., 12. Here Malcolm first begins to describe the "downward spiral" of his mother's emotional and mental health.

7 Ibid., 21.

8 Ibid. 26.

9 Ibid., 37.

Chapter Six: No Future without Forgiveness

1 Desmond Tutu, *No Future Without Forgiveness* (New York: Doubleday, 1997).

2 Ibid., 137. I could have chosen stories from the United States, but sometimes a bit of distance is necessary. Richard Lischer tells this story that resonates with the apartheid of South Africa, except that Lischer is describing Montgomery, Alabama: "In 1952, a white woman in Montgomery accused a Negro teenager of raping her. His name was Jeremiah Reeves, and he was a drummer in the Negro high-school band. A white court found him guilty and, after five years of legal appeals and protests, he was executed. . . . The entire city, from its magnolia-lined squares to its massive public buildings, churches, and monuments, was built on a carefully organized system of injustice." From *The Preacher King: Martin Luther King Jr. and the Word that Moved America* (New York: Oxford Press, 1995), 73.

3 Desmond Tutu, *No Future Without Forgiveness*, 137–141.

4   Another telling story of ca. 1950 Montgomery, Alabama, from Richard Lischer: "Despite the enforced intimacy of the races, a rigid caste system, buttressed by dozens of local statutes, forbade blacks and whites to acknowledge the life they in fact held in common. A local statute went so far as to bar whites and blacks from playing cards, dice, checkers, or dominoes together. Restrooms and drinking fountains were clearly marked. By law, a white person and a Negro could not share a taxi. The segregation of restaurants and public transportation was carried out with a routine cruelty that left the black citizens of Montgomery, like those of most southern cities, humiliated and burning with resentment" (*The Preacher King*, 72–73).

5   Elie Wiesel has spent much of his life pursuing the same ends. When he recently spoke at the church I pastor, he shared a brief anecdote I cannot forget. Following Nelson Mandela's release from prison, Wiesel held a reconciliation conference to which he invited the then President of South Africa, along with Mandela. After listening to Wiesel and Mandela describe the brutality of ethnic genocide and institutional racism, the young president stood up and declared to the entire audience, "I was born into apartheid; it's all I've ever known. My fervent wish is that I now am able to attend its funeral."

6   Desmond Tutu, *No Future Without Forgiveness*, 82–83.

7   Ibid., 137.

8   Frederick Buechner, *Wishful Thinking: A Theological ABC* (New York, Harper & Row, 1973), 2.

9   Jack Reese has written an important book regarding forgiveness and reconciliation for local churches: *The Body Broken* (Abilene, Texas: Leafwood Publishers, 2006).

10 Quoted in Philip Yancey's *What's So Amazing About Grace?* (Grand Rapids: Zondervan, 1997), 45. Yancey writes: "The Buddhist eight-fold path, the Hindu doctrine of karma, the Jewish covenant, and Muslim code of law—each of these offer a way to earn approval. Only Christianity dares to make God's love unconditional." N. T. Wright has written an important book about the subject of evil, justice, and forgiveness: *Evil and the Justice of God* (Downers Grove: InterVarsity Press, 2006). Wright's concluding chapter on forgiveness (in which he works with the contributions of Desmond Tutu and Miroslav Volf) is outstanding.

Chapter Seven: Suffering Can Be Beautiful

1   Gregory Stevenson is the author of *Televised Morality: The Case of Buffy the Vampire Slayer* (Lanham, Maryland: Hamilton Books, 2004).

2   Rodolfo Lanciana, *Ancient Rome in the Light of Recent Discoveries* (New York: Houghton Mifflin, 1888).

3   This point was inspired by Morna Hooker, "Believe and Follow: The Challenge of Mark's Ending," in *Preaching Mark's Unsettling Messiah*, Fleer and Bland, eds. (St. Louis: Chalice Press, 2006).

4   Story told by Dr. David Keller on September 21, 2007 at Michigan State University. "The Patsy" aired on February 21, 1960, as an episode of *General Electric Theatre*. You can see the episode's entry on the Internet Movie Database at http://www.imdb.com/title/tt0586346/.

5   C. S. Lewis has captured this truth in his novel, *Till We Have Faces: A Myth Retold* (New York: Harvest Publishing, 1956).

Chapter Eight: Professor Jack

1   The most helpful guide to understanding the current plight of Detroit is Thomas J. Sugrue's *The Origins of the Urban Crisis: Race and Inequality in Postwar Detroit* (Princeton: Princeton University Press, 1996).

2   Elie Wiesel, *Messengers of God* (New York: Simon & Schuster, 1985), 57.

3   I could not have written this chapter without the support of those who have worked in Cass Park with me: Kara, Emily, Emily D., Andy, Stephanie, Courtney, Jim, Amy, Mark, Matt, John, Becca, Joe, Erinn, Riley, and Mark.

Chapter Nine: A Place at the Table

1   Genesis 18 is, by the way, one of the best hospitality stories in all of Scripture.

2   Another source you might want to check out: *The Shack*, by William Young (Newbury Park, California: Windblown Media, 2007), is a novel that depicts God primarily through the lens of hospitality. It a superior portrayal of God's passion to welcome all to the prepared table.

3   Christine Pohl, *Making Room: Recovering Hospitality as a Christian Tradition* (Grand Rapids: Eerdmans, 1999). This is one of the most profound yet succinct treatments of hospitality in the history of Christianity.

4   Amy-Jill Levine, *The Misunderstood Jew: The Church and the Scandal of the Jewish Jesus* (New York: HarperOne, 2006), 149.

5   *Sight*, *see*, and *vision* are important words in Luke's Gospel. Read chapters 9–11 and 24:13–35 to see if I'm right.

6   Regarding the story of the Good Samaritan, I love this quote: "A true revolution of values will soon cause us to question the fairness and justice of many of our past and present policies. On the one hand, we are called to play the Good Samaritan on life's roadside, but that will be only an initial act. One day we must come to see that the whole Jericho Road must be transformed so that men and women will not be constantly beaten and robbed as they make

their journey on life's highway. True compassion is more than flinging a coin to a beggar. It comes to see that an edifice which produces beggars needs restructuring." Martin Luther King, Jr., at the Riverside Church in New York City on April 4, 1967, at a gathering of Clergy and Laity Concerned.

7 You can read Shane's original journals and reflections on The Simple Way, at http://www.thesimpleway.org/macro/shane_iraq.html.

8 I think my friend Randy Harris would say that times like these are reminders of the difference between *patriotism* and *nationalism*. A *patriot* honors what is honorable in one's country without turning a blind eye to the skeletons in the proverbial national closet (genocide, racism, slavery, greed, exploitation, etc.). A *nationalist* is loyal to king and country regardless of the ethical violations that might occur in order to make and keep one's country powerful.

Chapter Ten: Food and Water

1 See especially Acts 2:46.

2 Sara Miles, "Strangers Bring Us Closer to God," *All Things Considered*, 5 May 2008. You can read the online version of this episode at http://www.npr.org/templates/story/story.php?storyId=90133974. You might also enjoy a few films that explore the necessity of food in the process of redemption and reconciliation: *Babette's Feast* (1988), *Places in the Heart* (1984), *Cold Mountain* (2003), and *Antoine Fisher* (2002).

3 Rob Bell and Don Golden, *Jesus Wants to Save Christians: A Manifesto for the Church in Exile* (Grand Rapids: Zondervan, 2008), 180.

4 This idea starts with Paul in Romans 6. Bonhoeffer describes baptism in this way: "Baptism betokens a breach. Christ invades the realm of Satan, lays hands upon his own, and creates for himself his Church. By this act past and present are rent asunder." Dietrich Bonhoeffer, *The Cost of Discipleship* (New York: Simon & Schuster, 1959), 231.

5 As retold by my coworker in ministry, Dr. Patrick A. Mead, a.k.a. P-Middy.

6 Nicholas Sparks and Micah Sparks, *Three Weeks with My Brother: A Memoir* (New York: Time Warner, 2004), 288–293.

7 N. T. Wright, *Simply Christian: Why Christianity Makes Sense* (San Francisco: HarperSanFrancisco), 214–215.

Chapter Eleven: Keeping up with the Joneses

1 Apparently Paul reads *Moby Dick*. The latter part of this paragraph is from comments Walter Brueggemann made about that novel to a class I took with him at Columbia Seminary in the fall of 2008.

2 My friend John Laster pointed this out to me. See his interesting book, *Gaining Traction: Field Guide for Church Leadership* (St. Louis: Chalice Press, 2007).

3   Rachel Jones has written a great story about the work of God's Helping Hands in Auburn Hills, Michigan: "Hunger Hidden but Real in America's Suburbs," *All Things Considered*, originally aired November 22, 2005. You can read or listen to the program at http://www.npr.org/templates/story/story.php?storyId=5023760.

Chapter Twelve: An Invitation to Dance

1   "Out of Ur—Willow Creek Repents?" *Leadership Journal* blog, hosted on ChristianityToday.com, October 18, 2007. Read the original post at http://blog.christianitytoday.com/outofur/archives/2007/10/willow_creek_re.html.

2   Fred Craddock's comment from a Cherry Log Preaching Conference in the Spring of 2003 in Cherry Log, Georgia. Taken from my personal notes of his lecture.

3   I give credit to my friend and rabbi, John York, for this *New Living Nashville Translation*.

4   Lauren Winner, *Mudhouse Sabbath* (Brewster, Massachusetts: Paraclete Press, 2003), ix–x. People often misunderstand Judaism as "salvation by works." However, this fundamentally misinterprets the covenant relationship between Israel and YHWH. Because of their relationship, God expected them to behave in certain ways. Leviticus 19:18 ("Love your neighbor as yourself"), for instance, is one of the most powerful texts in all of Torah, even though it is embedded in an entire section of rules, commandments, and decrees. If one reads Leviticus 19:18 as the heart of this particular pericope, the advocacy becomes clear. While some insist that religion remain private (i.e. "Let's keep religion within the cult and private. Our duty is to simply keep the commandments of God."), others insist that "the rules are *passé*, leftover relics from the faith of our grandparents." The public element (public justice) is what is the heart of true Israelite religion. Leviticus 19 offers a third way, for it is concerned with obedience to the obligations set forth and the relationship of caring for the neighbor. That is, live in these particular ways (obeying relatively minute decrees) and once you find yourself in that cadence of spiritual habit, loving your neighbor will be the natural extension. If you will keep the strict dietary laws, etc., you will be able to have an open posture toward the "other." It will be impossible to have any invisible persons in your midst because you will be so attuned to God's presence.

5   Brian D. McLaren's *Finding Our Way: The Return of the Ancient Practices* (Nashville: Thomas Nelson, 2008), is an excellent introduction to spiritual formation and spiritual disciplines. As referenced in the Foreword, I interviewed McLaren regarding this book for *New Wineskins* in 2008. Read or listen at http://www.wineskins.org/filter.asp?SID=2&fi_key=149&co_key=1579.

6   Barbara Brown Taylor, *Leaving Church* (Boston: Cowley Press, 2005), 136–
137. Randy Harris loves to tell the story of Sandy Koufax, the great pitcher
from the Los Angeles Dodgers who chose not to pitch during Game One of
a World Series because it fell on the Jewish Day of Atonement (Yom Kippur).
When our identity as Christians (or Jews) trumps all other identities, then,
we will be fully invested in the right story.

7   See Walter Brueggemann's *Finally Comes the Poet: Daring Speech for
Proclamation* (Minneapolis: Fortress Press, 1989), 90–99. He also notes in
conversations regarding Sabbath and Jubilee that Sabbath is a "discipline"
that prepares people to do justice. You cannot truly love the poor and pray
for liberation if you are not willing to practice Sabbath. Sabbath is practiced
every seven days. The Year of Jubilee happens every forty-nine years. Social
justice, according to Brueggemann, is connected to personal devotion. The
two cannot be separated. Evidentially, the liberal and fundamentalist need
each other! "Sabbath," he writes, "is the end of grasping and therefore the
end of exploitation. Sabbath is a day of revolutionary equality in society. On
that day all rest equally, regardless of wealth or power or need" (Exodus 20:
8–11). Of course, the world is not now ordered according to the well-being
and equality of Sabbath rest. But the keeping of Sabbath, in heaven and on
earth, is a foretaste and anticipation of how the creation will be when God's
way is fully established." (*Interpretation: Genesis* [Louisville: Westminster
John Knox, 1982], 35–6). There is an intense relationship between piety and
social engagement all throughout the Hebrew Scriptures and into the New
Testament. To do one without the other, as I tell my students, is like trying
to dance with one leg. It can be done, but it's painful and awkward. Plus,
you'll run out of energy and quit. See Genesis 32; Isaiah 58:3–11; and Mark
12:28-34.

8   Thanks to my friend Greg Taylor for giving me this phrase during a car ride
in Tulsa, Oklahoma.

9   Eugene Peterson, *Eat This Book* (Grand Rapids: Eerdmans, 2006), 66.
Peterson also writes: "exegesis is an act of love. It loves the one who speaks
the words enough to want to get words right. It respects the words enough
to use every means we have to get the words right. Exegesis is loving God
enough to stop and listen carefully to what he says. It follows that we bring
the leisure and attention of lovers to this text, cherishing every comma and
semicolon, relishing the oddness of this preposition, delighting in the sur-
prising placement of this noun. Lovers don't take a quick look, get a 'message'
or a 'meaning,' and then run off and talk endlessly with their friends about
how they feel" (p. 55).

10 Many scholars go out of their way to point out that God's chief concern
regarding Israel's ethics in Deuteronomy and Leviticus was with the plight of
the poor and marginalized. Regarding Deuteronomy, Walter Brueggemann
claims, "The seductive land Israel is about to enter is transformable into

covenantal neighborhoods and this is how you do it: by caring for the alien, orphan, and widow. The Canaanite communities can be changed if these practices prescribed are met. Even the non-productive persons will not be invisible in the Israelite emerging economy of life" (from a lecture at Columbia Seminary, October 2008). For his take on justice in Leviticus, see "Justice as the Cornerstone: An Interpretation of Leviticus 18–20," *Interpretation 53* (1999), 341–50.

11 Donald Miller, *Blue Like Jazz: Non-Religious Thoughts on Christian Spirituality* (Nashville: Thomas Nelson, 2003), 122–125.

12 *Jim and Casper Go to Church: Frank Conversation about Faith, Churches, and Well-Meaning Christians* (Ventura, California: BarnaBooks, 2007).

Afterword: The Feast

1 Martin Luther King, "Eulogy of the Martyred Children," 1963. Access the speech in its entirety by at http://www.stanford.edu/group/King/publications/speeches/Eulogy_for_the_martyred_children.html.

2 See also John Mark Hicks' *Come to the Table: Revisioning the Lord's Supper* (Abilene, Texas: Leafwood Publishers, 2002).

THE FEAST

STUDY GUIDE

by Josh Ross

The Feast attempts to create a hunger for a holistic spirituality that is rooted in the Jesus Story. This is a move away from institutionalism and the temptation to compartmentalize the faith journey. Instead, it offers permission and a desperate invitation to yield to God as he cultivates imaginations that will rethink what it means to walk alongside neighbors and strangers as we embrace the character and nature of Jesus.

This study guide is important to *The Feast* because the content and stories in this book are meant for dialogue and action, not just for the downloading of information. Though the study guide can serve as a conduit for personal reflection, it is meant to function for small group settings.

Chapter 1
Making Sense of the Mess

Chapter Overview

Many of our churches have been transformed by cardboard testimonies, where individuals write their succinct before-and-after testimonies on two sides of a piece of cardboard, flipping it wordlessly before a watching congregation. After engaging in this powerful experience at my local church, a young man approached me wanting a few minutes of my time. Here were his words in a nutshell: "I'm not a believer in God and I've never been one. I'm twenty-three, and all I've known in life is drugs and gangs. I've moved from Michigan to Memphis for a fresh start. I didn't think I would be accepted here because of all my tattoos and the way I dress, but after what I experienced today, I think I could be a part of something like this. I could be a part of this kind of story." It is simple: people are drawn to authentic expressions of faith.

I find it interesting that Josh Graves begins a book entitled *The Feast* with the bizarre story tucked away in Genesis about a horny father-in-law and a desperate widow. In the opening book of the Bible, we see a thread that will weave its way throughout the pages of Scripture—that God has entered into the mess of life to love it and redeem it.

Digging Deeper _____

1) What does Genesis 38 tell us about God?

   a. A literal reading of the story reveals that God's role in this chapter is to "take out" the wicked brothers. When God's name appears, a death occurs. Is there something more on display here about the character and nature of God than the God who kills the wicked person? If so, what is it?

   b. Where is grace found in this story?

2) Take a moment to familiarize yourself with Genesis 37–39. What is the function of Genesis 38 in the Joseph narrative? What is the significance of this story in the book of Genesis?

3) _True or False_—Would you agree with Josh's following statement? "God isn't interested so much in people who look the part. God's interest lies in people who make a mess of the part."

   a. Reflect on this statement in light of Jesus' words in Luke 5:31–32: "Those who are well have no need of a physician, but those who are sick; I have come to call not the righteous but sinners to repentance."

   b. How do you find Luke 5:31–32 played out in the life of Jesus?

4) This chapter ends with the following claim, "God is interested in the messes we've made. God decides to enter into the mess, and makes sense of our world."

   a. Such a faith becomes a _way of life_ more than a component of a particular belief system, and this way of life is in opposition to many of our religious paradigms. How does this statement pose a threat to the present religious structures?

   b. If this statement were to become a lived reality, what challenges would it bring to those who want their religion clean, uninterrupted, organized, and consistent?

Local Context

1) John 1:14: "The Word became flesh and moved into the neighborhood." What would happen if the local church ceased to have conversations concerning who the target group is going to be when it comes to outreach and evangelism, and instead they decided to stand on the front porch of their church and welcome all those they see?

2) Do "messes" feel welcomed in your faith community?

3) What voice do you give to the mess in people's lives on a given Sunday during the worship service?

4) Reflect on this statement by evangelist Luis Palau, who captured the nature of the church in an earthly metaphor. The church, he said, is like manure. Pile it together and it stinks up the neighborhood; spread it out and it enriches the world.

Chapter 2
Theotokos

Chapter Overview

Should it come as a surprise that four foreign women are found in Matthew's genealogy? When we first discover these alien women who were all involved in some form of sexual scandal, we might be shocked by Matthew's inclusion of women who could jeopardize a list comprised of many God-anointed, God-appointed Jewish family members. However, after careful reflection on God's activity throughout the pages of Scripture, we shouldn't find it out of the norm to find God at work in the margins.

Digging Deeper

1) Read Matthew 1:18–24.

   a. What caught your attention when reading the text? What questions come to mind when reflecting on this story?

   b. Joseph had worked for years to become a *tsadiq*. This was a reputation that was earned, not inherited. How was Joseph's reputation at risk with the news of Mary's unexpected pregnancy?

   c. Josh writes, "Joseph trades his reputation for a new identity." How have you experienced the tension between reputation and identity in your own life?

2) What statement does God make by placing Jesus in the womb of a woman who "emerges out of a large segment in Israel known as the *anawim* (on-a-wheem), which simply means 'pious poor'"?

3) Consider the activity of God in the two births described by Luke in the beginning of his Gospel. They involve Zechariah and Elizabeth, whose reputations are on the line because they are old and barren, and also Joseph and Mary, whose reputations are on the line because they are engaged and expecting. What do see about God in these stories?

4) Josh states the following: "If the hardest place to live is right where we are, then where we are is the place from which we must begin." Reflect on the truth of this claim in your own life.

Local Context

1) Reflect on the same statement above, but this time reflect from the context of your local church, not your personal life: "If the hardest place to live is right where we are, then where we are is the place from which we must begin."

2) If you were to survey people from the neighborhood surrounding your church building concerning your reputation in the community, what responses would you receive?

3) Is your church invested in its surrounding community in such a way that the neighbors would weep if your leaders chose to move to another location?

Chapter 3
Wrestling with the Real Jesus

Chapter Overview

It is a store that has taken over shopping malls and has become a well-known place to celebrate young children's birthday parties. *Build-A-Bear* is more than just a store; it is an experience. The mission statement begins, "Our mission is to bring the Teddy Bear to life." As you work your way through this *bear-building* experience, you will find yourself going to stations, from Choose Me, to Hear Me, Stuff Me, Stitch Me, Fluff Me, Name Me, Dress Me, and Take Me Home. Essentially, you have the privilege of making a bear into whatever you want it to be. From its size to the clothing to the name, this bear is fashioned and formed in its owner's image. And so it is with Jesus. We have often dressed him up to fit into the world we have created. We have formed him into our belief systems, political parties, and worldviews. In Chapter 3, Josh addresses a critical problem: We have attempted to produce converts through salvation experiences that are often followed by indoctrination into a particular belief system—rather than *discipling* people into an alternative way of life where Jesus is revealed as the giver and sustainer of life. Tallying a convert-count is a byproduct of "Christian Consumerism," and it has become one of the greatest enemies of the church.

Digging Deeper _____

1) How have you created Jesus in your own image? Are you guilty of treating the life and teachings of Jesus as a spiritual buffet where

you pick and choose what components will fit into your life and what will be left out? How so?

2) Josh writes, "Deep prayer takes us to strange but holy places." We often talk as though prayer and communion with God are safe places to be. There is truth in this because God is a refuge, a strong tower, and a shelter. But also, the presence of God is one of the most dangerous places to be, not in a hellfire-and-brimstone kind of way, but because when we truly enter into *space* with God, we become vulnerable in the hands of the one who knows how to turn our worlds upside-down.

   a. Reflect on this—How is deep prayer with God both safe and dangerous?

   b. How have you experienced this tension?

3) "Thin spaces are the moments and places where heaven and earth kiss, where eternity, ever so subtly, creeps into our temporary lives." What "thin spaces" have you encountered recently?

4) Dallas Willard has coined the phrase "Vampire Christianity," the tendency to only want Jesus for his blood. How are you guilty of this?

5) Discuss the tension in being a fan, admirer, and believer in Jesus and being an authentic disciple of Jesus.

Local Context

1) Two major "measuring sticks" that churches use to gauge the health of their faith communities seem to be weekly attendance and weekly budget—two methods that tell us very little about the spiritual health of our people. How do we measure discipleship?

2) Do we believe that the gospel—the good news of Jesus—is truly the best news in the world, and if so, who is it good news for?

Chapter 4
The Greatest Risk

Chapter Overview

In this chapter, Josh admonishes the spirit of mediocrity. The good news of Jesus rebukes a spirituality of contentment and surface-level Christianity. The goal of following Jesus is not to become good, loyal citizens of an earthly kingdom. Instead, it is about becoming passionate Christ-followers who are not afraid to do daring things with their lives. In short, the gospel is for risk-takers.

Digging Deeper _____

1) What is meant by the phrase "Trumanist Christianity"? What has "trumanism" looked like in your own faith journey?

2) Read Matthew 25:14–30.

   a. Josh takes the position that "talents" are not about gifts or even money. He suggests that this is a parable about *not playing it safe*. It is about taking risks. Would you agree or disagree with Josh's interpretation? Why or why not?

3) We spend so much time in prayer praying for safety, security, and protection. Jesus didn't teach his followers to pray this way, and the church in Acts refused to water down Christianity to a "safe" way of life. When threatened in Acts 4, their prayer is for boldness.

a. How do we balance a life of safety and risk-taking?

b. How do Christ-followers raise their children in a way that empowers them to do something daring with their lives?

Local Context

1) Josh writes, "The greatest risk, in the economy of Christ, is to take no risk at all."

a. What becomes of the local church if they are driven by fear (fear of money, fear of numbers, fear of reputation, fear of losing out to the Joneses)?

b. What risks has your church taken to advance the kingdom?

2) Josh warns against escapism. Living the Jesus story is not about escaping from sinners, tax collectors, and outsiders. We are called to live as light and salt in a world hungry for the power of resurrection.

a. What are the benefits of escapism?

b. What are the downfalls?

3) Reflect on this quote by Pam Cope in her book *Jantsen's Gift*:

a. "The concept of a bad day for my kids is when the cable goes out, or there's not enough milk for their Lucky Charms. I want my kids to know a different life than that; to have a different understanding of what constitutes hardship. The best way for me to do this is to do what I regretted not having done for Jantsen: teach them, through the way I live my life, that the world is not as big as we think and it's my responsibility—and will someday be theirs—to take care of people who need our help, even if those people look nothing like us, or live someplace that seems far away and foreign. I see many of my friends trying to shield their kids from pain and disappointment the way that I did when Jantsen and Crista were young, but I can't continue to do that. I don't want them to be crippled by fear. I want them to take chances and live adventurous lives. I want them to live their dreams, and the best way I can teach them to do that is to let them watch me live mine."

Chapter Five
Can I Get a Witness?

Chapter Overview

Prophets are witnesses who speak from their experiences with God. Unlike Priests who work in the Temple, prophets become mouthpieces for God in the streets and marketplaces. The prophetic voice is considered bold and courageous but is almost always paired with great sacrifice. They have more enemies than allies. In this chapter, Josh explores the possibility of recovering the priestly and prophetic voice as essential to our faith journey. The power in these voices manifests itself through weakness, sacrifice, vulnerability, and deep commitment to an alternative story.

Digging Deeper _____

1) Josh begins the chapter by telling an extraordinary story of the power of acceptance after being the target of ridicule and abuse while attending a debate between Christian and Muslim ministers. He describes this experience by stating, "I felt as if I belonged to something spiritual, something *otherworldly*." When have you felt as though you belonged to something spiritual?

2) Read Jeremiah 7:3–7.

   a. What seems to be the primary function of a prophet?

    b. Josh suggests that the same charge brought against Israel concerning their allegiance to the Temple could also be made of modern Christianity in America. Would you agree with this assessment?

3) Nations have quickly claimed 2 Chronicles 7:14 to be a fulfilled prophesy of God's favor upon a particular group of people—"if my people who are called by my name will humble themselves, pray, seek my face, and turn from their wicked ways, then I will hear from heaven, and will forgive their sins and heal their land."

    a. Who are the "we" and the "their" in this passage? What is your reaction to Lee Camp's statement that the "we" and "their" should refer to the church, not a political party or particular form of government?

    b. Is 2 Chronicles 7:14 a prophesy concerning a particular nation on earth?

4) Reflect on these words from Josh: "The United States, according to the witness of Scripture, is more like Assyria, Babylon, or Rome, jockeying for position on the world stage, controlling nations for her own interest."

Local Context

1) If Jesus was determined to set up Christianity as *the* primary religion of a particular nation on earth, why did he not spend more time in courts, palaces, and in the presence of kings and rulers, instead of spending most of his time in small, rural towns?

2) Was Christianity ever meant to function as the primary religion of an earthly kingdom?

Chapter Six
No Future without Forgiveness

Chapter Overview

Desmond Tutu was receiving an honorary doctorate at Emory University, and he began to thank the people who had been praying during the struggles with apartheid in his homeland. He mentioned a nun who had been praying nightly for him in the Bay Area. He said, "Here I am, being prayed over every night for three decades at 2:00 in the morning by a nun I don't know standing in a patch of woods in northern California. What chance does the apartheid government in Africa stand against that?"

In this chapter, Josh portrays God as unpredictable. Josh has a long list of biblical witnesses to back up his argument that God often connects with us through unassuming people and unexpected experiences. Josh's friend Benny is not alone when he discovers that connecting with God sometimes feels as though our prayers are bouncing off a ceiling. In these moments, we learn that prayer is not always about getting what we want, but it is about being formed into His glorious image. Praying with our eyes closed draws us nearer to the God of intimacy and mystery. Praying with our eyes open teaches us that we are intricately involved in God's rhythm of creation. Through unassuming people and unexpected places, we begin to see people as image-bearers of God himself, and when this takes place, reconciliation and the naming of sins become vital components to living lives of Spirit-filled community.

Digging Deeper

1) If God is all-powerful and all good, why does evil exist?

   a. How has God defeated evil?

   b. What roles do *forgiveness* and *reconciliation* play in defeating evil in our present context? (Note the impact of the Truth and Reconciliation Commission in South Africa.)

2) How do you see yourself as a participating member of dysfunction, sin, and injustice, and how does this keep you from the redeeming process of healing and change?

3) Read 2 Corinthians 5:16–21.

   a. What is the connection between "new creation" (5:17) and "ministers of reconciliation" (5:18–19)?

   b. How do our baptisms involve us in God's redeeming work throughout all of creation?

4) Josh makes this claim, "The Bible is the real world." He is not referring to the Bible as a history book, but as the story of God that is still relevant to the culture we live in. We've all heard the prayer at the end of a worship service that goes like this—"God, be with us as we leave this place and enter into the *real world*." How has this understanding of "the real world" depleted our understanding of God's activity around us?

Local Context

1) In her book, *Speaking of Sin*, Barbara Brown Taylor writes, "In many congregations, the only sins openly denounced from the pulpit are low attendance, poor stewardship, and failure to sign up for Sunday school."

   a. What is the language of sin in your church?

b. What opportunities are provided for people in your local church to speak openly about sin in their lives?

2) Reflect on this statement by Josh in regard to your own church culture: "More important than sums of money or prison sentences is the need for reconciliation between flesh-and-blood humans whose eyes must meet despite the pain brewing inside."

Chapter 7
Suffering Can Be Beautiful

Chapter Overview

It would be interesting to put this chapter in conversation with the *The Prayer of Jabez* by Bruce Wilkinson or the prosperity gospel theology of Joel Osteen for a friendly round table discussion. Most Americans are more interested in "suffering eliminated" or "suffering avoided" than they are in "suffering made beautiful." Though many faith communities strangle the questions that are haunting people concerning suffering and faith, Jesus comes as the ultimate sufferer. Scripture testifies to the truth that suffering gives birth to resurrection, redemption, good news, and meaningful life.

Digging Deeper _____

1) After telling the story of Sally's journey to America, Josh makes this claim: "Suffering can be redemptive." How was this true in Sally's life? How has it been true in your life?

2) Reread Isaiah 52:3–7 to catch the vastness of the phrase, "How beautiful are the feet . . ."

   a. "Your God reigns." It was a one-sentence sermon that told the people everything they needed to know. What did these words declare to Israel?

   b. Reflect on the power of the declaration in your own faith
       community.

3) Where is God's reign in your life?

4) The reign of God exists in opposition to other kingdoms of this
   world. Eugene Peterson writes, "The kingdom we are participating in when we pray, 'Your kingdom come,' is not in competition
   with the kingdoms of America or IBM or Honda or Microsoft. It
   is subverting them!"

   a. What other kingdoms have you sworn your allegiance to on
       earth?

   b. What one thing in your life needs to be given over to the
       Lordship of Jesus in order for God's reign to flourish within
       you?

Local Context

1) Where is God's reign evident in your local church?

2) Where is his reign lacking?

Chapter 8
Professor Jack

Chapter Overview

In Chapter 6, Josh made the claim that God often connects with us through unassuming people and unexpected experiences. In Chapter 8, Josh bears witness to this reality. Only Jesus can bring together a white suburbanite and a working homeless man from the inner city. This chapter is more than the cultivation of a relationship of two people from opposite worlds; it is about a thin space where God works His wonders.

Digging Deeper _____

1) Professor Jack spoke these piercing words: "Make us feel *real*. We want to feel like we are real people."

    a. When do you feel most alive in your walk with God?

    b. What makes you feel real?

    c. How does your life make other people feel real?

2) Reflect on this statement by Barbara Brown Taylor: "Humans do not lose control. We lose the illusion that we were ever in control in the first place."

3) Concerning hospitality, Josh writes, "Until we follow this aspect of Jesus' life, going from host to hosted, we will miss out on the

true power of God's way in our lives." Do you find it easier to host or to be the one hosted?

4) Read Matthew 25:31–46.

   a. What is the most challenging aspect of this story?

   b. What do these words tell us about Jesus and his mission in the world?

Local Context

1) Many people care about the poor; they just don't know the poor. One of the greatest lessons God has taught me over the last decade is that the homeless and the poor have names; they have stories. How has this lesson been taught in your church?

2) What is your church's relationship with the poor in your city?

3) Reflect on *communal hospitality*. What does it mean to be a church that practices hosting and being hosted?

Chapter 9
A Place at the Table

Chapter Overview

Josh explores the power of the question that has transformed pews, living rooms, and kitchen tables. The question "Who is my neighbor?" can be haunting to say the least. It spoke straight to the heart of the lawyer in Luke 10, and it continues to poke at our invite-lists today. Josh broadens the definition of hospitality by arguing that it is more than handshakes or even table fellowship; it is about our lives mingling with people all around us. This is the way of Jesus.

Digging Deeper _____

1) Read Luke 10:25–37.

   a. What are the different ways people have interpreted this passage?

   b. Josh quotes one thinker as writing, "We should think of ourselves as the person in the ditch and then ask, 'Is there anyone from any group, about whom we'd rather die than acknowledge, *She offered help* or *He showed compassion*.'?" Who would be that person for you?

2) The lawyer asks a good question: "Who is my neighbor?" The resurrection of Jesus reframes the question in this way: "Who

is not my neighbor?" How are relationships with coworkers and strangers changed by this perspective?

3) How do we "universalize our definition of neighbor"?

4) What is the most difficult component of *welcoming strangers*?

5) Whom do you allow to enter into the inner places of your life?

Local Context

1) Josh states, "Hospitality is about welcoming those who do not have family or friends." What is the significance of this statement, good and bad, in your local church?

2) Toward the end of the chapter, Josh says, "The places everyone else ran from were the places we believed God was calling us to run toward. If others ran from the projects, from the homeless, from single moms, from skateboarders with drug problems—we ran to them." Are your leaders and ministers willing to follow Jesus to the dangerous places of your community and neighborhood?

Chapter 10
Food and Water

Chapter Overview

Baptism is more than a get-out-of-hell-free card, and the Lord's Supper is more than a memorial in which we mourn the death of Jesus. These two spiritual practices are used by God to prepare us to live as his people between Sundays. They make us come alive. In this chapter, Josh argues that baptism and the Lord's Supper are essential to the life of a Christ-follower, because these two practices orient us into the story of God. We live and love differently because we have been in the waters and have shared in the bread and cup. Through these practices, intimacy with God is deepened, relationships with people are cultivated, and participation in God's work in the world is demanded.

Digging Deeper

1) Take a few moments to think about your baptism.

   a. What do you remember? Who was there? What do you remember thinking as you went into the water?

   b. What powerful baptisms have you witnessed?

2) In his book *The Body Broken*, Jack Reese states that the New Testament argues *from* baptism more than it argues *for* baptism. You will have a difficult time finding in Scripture where Paul, Peter, or any other writer makes the claim, "This is why you

need to be baptized." This is because every New Testament book is written to baptized believers. When the authors talk about baptism, they are always saying, "Because you have been baptized, this is the kind of life you are called to live." This is true in Romans 6, 1 Corinthians 12, Galatians 3, Ephesians 4, Colossians 2, and more. The goal of baptism is to live a new life.

   a. What is your baptism calling you to *today*?

   b. In light of your baptism and your participation in the bread and cup, where is God calling you to become more?

3) Do you agree with Josh's assertion, "When people gather to eat Jesus' meal, they are making a political and social statement?" Why or why not?

4) What must change in your life if you choose to wake up every day considering, "Today, I choose to live as a baptized person"?

Local Context

1) How does the "food and water" discussed in this chapter transform the way we see the world and interact with our neighbors?

2) How does the church come together to live as a baptized group of people who have been ushered into a movement?

Chapter 11
Keeping Up with the Joneses

Chapter Overview

To choose to follow Jesus is to swear an allegiance to his kingdom where he is Lord of all. Jesus comes for our hearts, souls, minds, and wallets. The Franks used to baptize their military soldiers with their right hands—the hand that held the sword—sticking out of the water. They were willing to surrender nearly all of their lives to Jesus, but they had to be able to kill at will. For many of us today, it is not our sword-bearing hands we are holding out of the waters of baptism, it is our wallets. Three times in the Gospel of Luke, Jesus makes preposterous demands for people to sell what they have and give to the poor. This chapter creatively portrays a conversation that takes place concerning Paul's bold claim in 1 Timothy 6:10, "For the love of money is a root of all kinds of evil. Some people, eager for money, have wandered away from the faith and pierced themselves with many griefs" (NIV).

Digging Deeper

1) What do you make of the following statistics?:

   a. Poor people in the United States give more than the wealthy.

   b. Out of the twenty-two "industrialized nations" of the world, the United States ranks *dead last* in regard to her capacity to give versus what citizens actually give.

c. Americans spend more than four hundred *billion* dollars on Christmas every single year. For only ten billion, we would be able to provide the entire world with clean drinking water.

d. The average churchgoer in the United States gives less than three percent of his or her annual income to church.

2) Who are people you know who have used their wealth for kingdom-significance?

3) What keeps you—what is holding you back—from being a joyful giver?

4) What does it mean for Jesus to become the Lord of everything we own? Closets? Living rooms? Kitchens? Cars? Roth IRAs? Savings Accounts?

5) Read Luke 18:18–30.

a. What strikes you as strange about this story?

b. Is Jesus really asking this man to relinquish all of his possessions, or is he just telling him to get his priorities straight?

c. What is the "one thing" that you need to let go of in order to follow Jesus?

Local Church

1) Reflect on Luke 18:18–30 as a conversation between Jesus and your local church. What is the "one thing" your church needs to let go of to receive these words from Jesus concerning authentic discipleship?

2) In what ways does the desire to build bigger barns and empires keep us from being involved in our surrounding communities and neighborhoods?

Chapter 12
An Invitation to Dance

Chapter Overview

A recurring claim in *The Feast* is that the power of Jesus seeks to do more than produce mere converts; Christ bids us to become followers, imitators, and apprentices. In the words of Dietrich Bonhoeffer, "When Christ calls a man, he bids him come and die." In a book that bids people to follow Jesus into unexpected places, it is necessary to end with healthy instructions on maintaining a spiritual life through disciplines that draw us into the rhythm of God. We must work with God to develop practices that sustain our faith journey.

Digging Deeper _____

1) What spiritual disciplines sustain you?

2) Reflect on the significance of the confession made by Bill Hybels in the beginning of this chapter.

3) In salvation, we are saved *from* something and *into* something.

   a. What have you been saved from?

   b. What have you been saved into?

4) Josh defines spiritual disciplines as "the daily means by which we come into contact with God." He touches on the following disciplines:

    a. Sabbath

    b. Exercise

    c. Reading

    d. Giving

    e. Solidarity with the poor

    f. Confession

5) How have the disciplines listed above helped you connect with God?

6) What disciplines would you add?

Local Context

1) What spiritual disciplines are sustaining your local church?

2) What expectations has your church established for new members concerning their pursuit of the life of Jesus?

About the Author

Joshua Graves is the preaching and teaching minister for the Otter Creek Church in Nashville, Tennessee. He is currently a doctoral student at Columbia Seminary, studying the relationship of postmodernism and Christianity. In addition to other articles and essays, Josh also wrote the study guide for *Mere Discipleship* (Brazos Press, 2008). Josh is married to Kara—the daily source of joy in his life and the real theologian in the family. They have one son, Lucas. You can read his blog at www.joshgraves.blogspot.com.